AMERICA,
BUT
BETTER

CHRIS CANNON &
BRIAN CALVERT

AMERICA,

BUT BETTER

The **CANADA PARTY** *MANIFESTO*

Douglas & McIntyre
D&M PUBLISHERS INC.
Vancouver/Toronto/Berkeley

Douglas & McIntyre
An imprint of D&M Publishers Inc.
2323 Quebec Street, Suite 201
Vancouver BC Canada V5T 4S7
www.douglas-mcintyre.com

Cataloguing data available from Library and Archives Canada
ISBN 978-1-77100-062-8 (paperback)
ISBN 978-1-77100-063-5 (ebook)

Editing by Trena White
Copyediting by Peter Norman
Cover and text design by Peter Cocking
White Haven illustration by Ryan Heshka
Printed and bound in Canada by Friesens
Distributed in the U.S. by Publishers Group West

We gratefully acknowledge the financial support of the Canada Council for the Arts, the British Columbia Arts Council, the Province of British Columbia through the Book Publishing Tax Credit, and the Government of Canada through the Canada Book Fund for our publishing activities.

WE WISH TO DEDICATE this book to the American citizen, whose forebears ushered the world into an age of democracy and enlightenment, whose grandparents risked everything to preserve these ideals through the most brutal wars the world has ever known, who today march, protest, occupy, and sacrifice to leave a better world for their children. We are behind you. Don't fuck it up.

CONTENTS

4 Treating Experts like Mammals:
An Ideological Throwdown! *105*

FOREWORD
BY ABRAHAM LINCOLN

FOUR-SCORE AND sixty-seven years ago, I was watching a dreadful performance of *Our American Cousin*, wishing I were dead. I hate the theater.

And then a funny thing happened.

I can't help but wonder if I might have survived that night if my government had free health care, a more reasonable policy of gun control, a mastery of the apology, or even a national hockey program to help the North and South settle their differences on the ice.

It has been two centuries and some change since our fathers brought forth on this continent a new nation, conceived in liberty and dedicated to the proposition that all men—and eventually women—are created equal. But now we are engaged in a great uncivil war that threatens to test whether that nation, so far removed from the founding principles upon which it was conceived and dedicated, can long endure.

I believed in my lifetime that the cure to a divided America rested in the hands of the North. Today our solution lies just a bit farther, in the hands of the good people who occupy the true North, strong and free. Within these pages lies the blueprint for our future, a nation returned to the principles of liberty and equality, plus some stuff about hockey. Perhaps if we had this book in my lifetime, I should not have perished from this earth.

ABRAHAM LINCOLN
Penny Aficionado,
Sixteenth President of the United States

INTRODUCTION

HELLO, AMERICA. It's us, Canada. You might remember us from the documentary *Strange Brew*. Or that flag you sewed onto your backpack the summer you bummed around Europe. Or that time in the sixties when your hippies slid into us like second base, waiting until it was safe to return home.

But we're more than the country you kick in your sleep as you slumber through the American Dream. We're your next-door neighbor, and the paper-thin border has done little to muffle the sound of your political anguish. We tried turning up the stereo, but every other song is Bryan Adams, which just makes the headaches worse.

So we're pursuing the only option left: We want you to elect us the next President of the United States. We had a chat with the rest of the world, and everyone agrees your addiction to dangerous, divisive politics has gotten out of hand, and you're headed for an overdose. We're offering you the chance to kick back for a while and let a trusted friend cook your meals and fluff your pillows, giving you time to do some healing and generally reevaluate your place in the universe. So this is not an invasion; it's an intervention.

Why are we qualified to lead America? Because we are America Jr., the little brother who has idolized you since we were baby colonies spitting up in Britain's lap. We've grown up together, tamed a frontier together, laughed, cried, bled, overeaten at Thanksgiving, and conquered outer space together. We share the same spacious skies and amber waves of grain, the same purple mountain majesties, the same sea to the same shining sea.

Sure, we've had a few rough patches. The War of 1812. Vietnam. Celine Dion.* But we've weathered these storms to develop the largest trading partnership, most integrated militaries, and weakest beers in the known universe. Both of our Constitutions are based on the personal liberties outlined in Mom's Magna Carta, and it is this—our mutual status as beacons of freedom to the rest of the world—that unites us in cause and makes us continental BFFs.

Which is why it has been with great sadness, and more than a little nausea, that we've witnessed our American brothers and sisters betrayed over the past decade by privately owned politicians who have created franchises out of persecuting the disenfranchised, fetishized ignorance at the expense of reason, deprived citizens of their civil liberties in the name of a very profitable notion of security, and driven up taxpayer debt to finance solid gold pockets to carry their other gold.

---

* Again, we are really, *really* sorry about that.

We have watched from a distance with the same horrified stare one might impart on a busload of kittens being carried away by a tornado. We have watched class warfare committed by classless bourgeoisie. We have watched as huddled masses yearning to breathe free were told that it is un-American to huddle, mass, yearn, or breathe. We have watched, and for years have asked ourselves, "Isn't somebody going to help those poor folks!?"

And then we realized: *We* are a somebody. And we're not just an "outside the beltway" candidate, we're outside the border. So we've written this book—translated from Canadian to American English—to explain our platform and convince you that you're better off getting an overhaul from an honest mechanic than being scrapped by China and sold for parts.

America used to be the world's quarterback—popular, hardworking, and ruggedly handsome, the country everyone aspired to be. But then there was that White House party the new administration kicked off in 2000. Remember that? Pissed-off neighbors? Carpets stained with motor oil? All the rent money spent on beer and airport groping? America stopped playing with the team, got fat and lazy, started beating up gays and hassling women, becoming the bully that other countries fear but don't respect. And Canada, a few years your junior, got dragged down with you, our self-esteem—although many of us will deny it—intimately tied to that of our older brother. We told you not to drink and drill. But you didn't listen. And now we are all paying the price.

It's not like we don't have our own faults. Our prime minister makes Dick Cheney look like a human-rights crusader. Our oil program is so apocalyptic it was given a "Special Thanks" credit in the book of Revelations. And we have recently earned permanent-member status in the election-fraud club coveted by up-and-coming superpowers the world over. Which is why, once we become your president, we will turn around and invade ourselves, as we could use a good regime change of our own.

But since it's colder in Canada, the concepts of freedom and neighborliness have been kept fresher. Liberty is still crisp. And although our own leadership has left the refrigerator door open and begun rotting the ideals that sustain us, a daunting opportunity has surfaced with the rise of the oil sands and the melting of the Northwest Passage, and we now face the terrifying prospect of becoming a superpower in our own right.

But we don't want to do it alone. We still love you, America. You are family. We want to remain brothers, side by side down the longest border in the world, a border marked by a monument inscribed with the words "May These Gates Never Be Closed." We would like the same to be true of our minds, which is why we're asking you to elect us your leader.

We are aware that your laws say presidential candidates have to be U.S.-born, but since Canada recognizes the rights of same-continent partners, we are legally obligated to declare ourselves a U.S. citizen by proxy. So instead of marking the box for "Most Charming Hypocrite," why not vote for the country you deserve? We are the Canada Party, and we want to help you rebuild the great nation this world sorely needs: America, but better.

The
CANADA PARTY
MANIFESTO

REALLY
IMPORTANT
MAPS

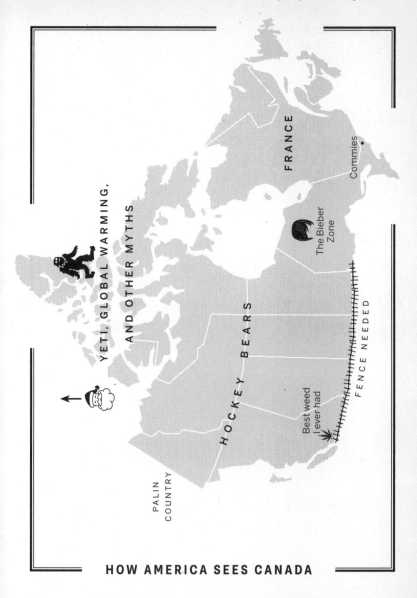

YETI, GLOBAL WARMING, AND OTHER MYTHS

FRANCE

Commies

The Bieber Zone

HOCKEY BEARS

FENCE NEEDED

Best weed I ever had

PALIN COUNTRY

HOW AMERICA SEES CANADA

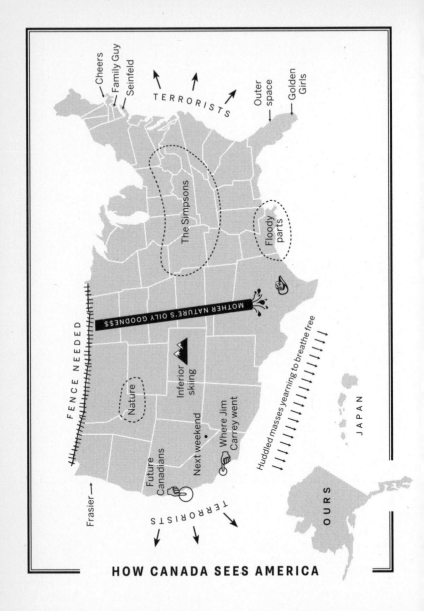

HOW CANADA SEES AMERICA

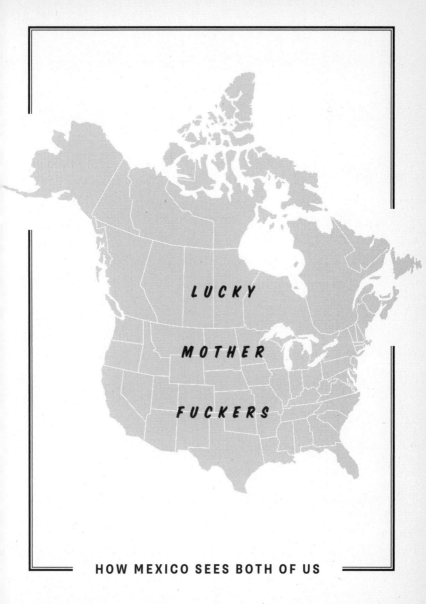

HOW MEXICO SEES BOTH OF US

AMERICA AND CANADA
CONTINENTAL BFFS

1.1 Timeline of U.S.-Canadian History

1775: "Awkward Autumn" becomes the theme at the annual British Empire family portrait when America and Canada show up wearing the same flag.

1776: America signs the Declaration of Independence, kicking their war with Britain into high gear. Canada, not wanting to offend anybody, fights for both sides.

1776–80: Thousands of British Loyalists in the U.S. move north to Canada, still largely a British colony. A fur trapper is trampled to death at the Hudson's Bay Company's first ever Boxing Day sale. Bryan Adams begins his music career.

1789: Pennsylvania ends its prohibition of theatrical performances, allowing the signing of the Constitution and the centuries of drama it would incur.*

---

* Although drafted while medicine was theoretical and man-tights all the rage, it is still referenced literally in modern American law.

1812: A young America acts out its own colonial fantasy and invades future-Canada, then retreats, realizing a new driveway is not worth the roaming charges.*

1814: British forces capture Washington, D.C., and burn it to the ground, although the pubs and bordellos remain curiously untouched.

1815: Britain finalizes the Treaty of Ghent after losing a round of Beer Pong. Well played, America. Well played.

1830–60: Tens of thousands of American slaves "emigrate" to Canada via the Underground Railroad, which is sort of like a Disney ride with less racism.

1861–65: American Civil War. Canada invents popcorn and takes to the sidelines.

1867: Three British colonies unite to form an independent Canada. American newspaper headlines exclaim: "Whatever."

1901: A government census shows 3.5 percent of Canadians were born in America and 1.6 percent of Americans were born in Canada. When asked why they emigrated, the majority of respondents on both sides checked the box marked "Looking for hotter women."

1907: The USS *Nashville* sails into the Great Lakes without asking. Canada apologizes for getting in the way, pays for dinner.

---

* Exactly two hundred years later we get around to writing this book.

1921: Canada develops a defensive strategy to repel a U.S. invasion. Canadians are instructed to "act normal" to avoid detection.

1939: Canada calls King George VI, politely asking permission to declare war on Germany. The king replies, "Who is this?"

1941: America and Canada cooperate to send 133,000 of their citizens to internment camps as part of a Japanese Community Outreach Program.

1945: At the end of World War II, Canada possesses the fourth-largest air force and third-largest naval surface fleet in the world. America giggles, calls it "cute."

1958: America and Canada finally agree on the curtain color for the NORAD underground bunker.

1960s: Canadians, having already experienced a Toronto garbage strike during a heat wave, avoid entering the Vietnam War. Fifty thousand Americans move to Canada, giving rise to bong-craft's "Glazed Age."

1972: Canada realizes Richard Nixon is a Dick.

1974: America realizes Richard Nixon is a dick, pretend they noticed first.

1988: Canadian hockey great Wayne Gretzky is traded from the Edmonton Oilers to the Los Angeles Kings. Canada mourns, and learns that California has a hockey team.

1994: The North American Free Trade Agreement (NAFTA) encourages trade between America, Canada, and Mexico. Canada and Mexico discover neither of them has anything the other wants.

2008: Canadian Justin Bieber is discovered on YouTube, instantly becoming an international celebrity—a far cry from his high-school nickname of "Singing-and-Dancing Pussy Boy."

2010: Canada defeats the U.S. in Olympic men's hockey, winning the gold medal in overtime. Awesome.

2012: Canada is elected President of the United States. Global warming abruptly ends as the atmosphere's greenhouse gases are blown into space when the entire planet exhales a collective sigh of relief.

1.2 Grok the Vote: Campaign Reform for Idiots

THERE IS perhaps no reform Americans would appreciate more than a Canadian approach to the election process. Like a summer-camp love affair, a Canadian election is passionate, awkward, a legal maximum of three months, and regularly punctuated by rainy afternoons doing arts-n-crafts. The longest election cycle in Canadian history was 74 days, when Liberal candidate William Lyon Mackenzie King defeated the

IT'S A PROMISE!

☞ Pay rates for Congress and the Senate will be directly tied to their productivity. Bonuses will be awarded for responsible governance. Penalties will carry the same interest as student loans.

Conservative Party's Arthur Meighen in 1926. (The Progressive Party came in third, and was awarded a yellow ribbon and a Tim Hortons gift certificate.)

Watching American elections through the CNN peephole, Canada sees something that resembles a room of diarrhetic chimps holding a year-long shit-tossing-themed house party that makes one forget the original wall color. For the 2012 presidential contest, Newt "Moon Tang Clan" Gingrich declared his candidacy nineteen months before the election. One-third of Canada's prime ministers have spent less time than that actually holding the office.

If the U.S. federal election process was not already a national

⚜ CANAFACT

Canada's election cycle has a thirty-six-day legal minimum. Candidates spend most of that time apologizing to the other candidates for the inconvenience.

exercise in waste and bad haircuts, the 2010 Citizens United decision by the Supreme Court—declaring that unrestricted political spending is protected by the First Amendment—has turned it into a full-on Trump family reunion. Estimates for 2012 election expenditures top $10 billion, more than twenty times the annual budget of the Corporation for Public Broadcasting, which is the favorite example of waste and bad haircuts held up by many of the politicians benefiting from this money.

The longer and more costly the election process, the more polarized and polarizing the voters become. The level of unity-inducing paranoia in federal elections may soon lead to four-year cycles of real-estate markets catering exclusively to political demographics.

To prevent U.S. elections from becoming a self-sustaining industry financed by fear and nonrecyclable yard signs, while simultaneously addressing the growing disconnect between citizen and candidate, we propose bringing voters and votees together for a little one-on-one through our new, streamlined election process, Speed Voting.

Based on the practice of speed dating, Speed Voting will give every interested citizen a fifteen-second face-to-face with each candidate, during which they can ask whatever they want. The rounds will be televised and made available, unedited, on an elections website, searchable by categories such as geography, platform, hilarity, and stutter duration. Replacing the role of independent investigator once entrusted to—and recently abandoned by—the mainstream media, Speed Voting will match the fifteen-second span of the typical sound bite, which is also the average time a voter spends researching any particular topic. For many, Speed Voting will present an exciting chance to smell a millionaire. For others, an opportunity to photobomb a soon-to-be-jailed United States senator.

There will, of course, still be debates to confuse and entertain the masses. To reengage young voters in the political process, we have designed this handy drinking game (on the next page) so they can play along.*

---

* We recommend playing with Canadian beer to provide actual intoxication.

The Canada Party Official "Grok the Vote" Drinking Game

- A candidate invokes the Founding Fathers to address an issue that didn't exist before 1972: Take a drink.

- A candidate cites the Constitution to back a point contrary to what the Constitution actually says: Take a drink.

- A candidate mispronounces a country with whom the U.S. is at war: Take a drink.

- A candidate says he wants to get the government out of your private life, and then argues against contraception or gay marriage in the same sentence: Take a drink.

- A candidate complains about the unfair treatment of white people: Take a drink.

- A candidate attacks the moderator for asking a fair question: Take a drink.

- A moderator apologizes for asking a fair question: Take two drinks.

- A candidate cites the teachings of Jesus in an argument against helping the poor: Take a drink.

- An audience member makes a racist statement during the Q&A: Take a drink and slap yourself.

- A candidate fails to correct the racist statement because it works in his favor: Take a drink and slap the person on your right. If that person is of a different race, do a "Hate Crime Shot" (waterboard yourself with tequila).

- A candidate disparages Canada's health care: Take a drink and move to Canada.

- A candidate provides an informed, fair, and practical solution to a complex problem: Consume remaining alcohol and exit the holodeck.

1.3 **Making English the Official Language for Native English Speakers**

....

MORE THAN three hundred languages are spoken in the United States, and let's be honest, none of them are as lovely as the Queen's English. The language of commerce and conquest, of Shakespeare and Dorothy Parker, of CSI: *Las Vegas*, CSI: *Miami*, and CSI: NY. Truly a global tongue.

> **CANAFACT**
> In 1969, Canada declared French the country's second official language. To express appreciation, Quebec outlawed English.
> ....

For decades, Americans have been locked in a bitter struggle over whether to make English the country's *official* language, so that alien invaders, when they decide to conquer earth, can avoid an embarrassing breach of interstellar protocol when they land on the White House lawn, slither down the flying-saucer ramp, and mistakenly utter the words "*Llévame a su líder.*"

Beyond interstellar matters, the philosophical stakes are what really drive the debate: whether or not citizens who don't speak English should be allowed to vote, drive cars, and understand signs warning of possible shark attacks. Clearly a battle to save America's soul.

Judging by the number of students enrolled in ESL (English as a Second Language) courses in the U.S.—about 3.8 million, accounting for 11 percent of the entire student population—even immigrants agree. That's why we wholeheartedly endorse a constitutional amendment making English the official language of the United States of America. That's also why this new amendment will require every American to pass our EPL (English as a Primary Language) course. Sample lessons include:

- "Where You At?": Grammar That Breaks the Heart

- "Let's Eat, People!": How Commas Can Prevent a Zombie Apocalypse

- "Your Welcome": Homonyms That Will Make People Stop Thanking You

- Using "Like" as an Adverb: Why People, Like, Want to Kill You When You Do That

- Irregardless, Orientate, and Other Words That Reflect on Your Value as a Human Being

In addition to written quizzes, all citizens will be required to pass oral exams to demonstrate a basic grasp of diction and pronunciation. For instance, when you utter the phrase "We will use nukes to fight terrorism," the audience should not be hearing the word "tourism." It confuses the terrorists and frightens the tourists. Similarly, words like "nother," "probly," "jewlry," and "maynaise" will be airlifted to the island of lost syllables for a tearful reunion. It will be illegal for anyone to "aks" someone a question except in direct homage to *Futurama*.

We will build special reeducation facilities for people who pronounce "America" as if it has only two syllables. The United States is a proud country, with proud vowels. It doesn't need a nickname. However, as French is the principal tongue of Quebec and Canada's second official language, we will honor French speakers by allowing an apostrophe-riddled

IT'S A PROMISE!

☞ American English and Canadian English will be combined to form some sort of Super English that wears a cape and shoots lasers out of its punctuation.

form of the title when it appears in print. Because ignoring the diversity of our community, as most U.S. citizens will tell you, would be downright un-'mer'can.

1.4 Combining Our Cities: Welcome to Van Francisco, Dirty Hippie Capital of the World!

REDUCING THE political divide between Canada and the United States would be pointless if we didn't also address the cultural divide. Just as children must learn to share their toys when they live in the same room, our nations must learn to share their urban spaces when they team up to be the best damn country Jesus and Santa Claus ever imagined.

> ❦ **CANAFACT**
> Americans can become born-again Canadians by accepting hockey into their life and dipping their forehead into a bowl of maple syrup.

We propose integrating American and Canadian cities to form somewhat virtual megacities, largely connected by the internet, high-speed rail, and a vague sense of something familiar off in the distance. Although tempted to pair cities using the "odd couple" plot device (the Chinatown of the North meets the swamp people of Florida), we opted instead to create positive partnerships that contribute to the nation as a whole.

Van Francisco
CITY MOTTO: *"Prohibere faciens me furere"* ("Quit harshing my mellow.")
BIGGEST IMPORT: UV lamps
BIGGEST EXPORT: Synonyms for "wet"

Imagine the power of combining San Francisco's caffeinated, tech-savvy hippies with Vancouver's outdoorsy, weed-savvy hippies. Interstate 5 would become the world's largest bike lane. Facebook would stop trying to improve itself and "just be grateful for what it has." Granola would become a verb. Ultimate Frisbee would finally be considered a sport.

This new breed of super-hippie would consolidate North America's sense of righteous indignation into a single, uniform voice for oppressed people no one has actually ever met. Berkeley would establish its long-awaited "Department of *Simpsons* References," and "Mr. Plow" would become the school fight song. A well-funded system of communes would shelter the entire homeless population, where they would find meaning and personal fulfillment turning unused city plots into organic crack farms.

Queboston

POPULATION: Who's askin'?

SPORTS TEAM: The Rouge Sox

OFFICIAL FOOD: Anything fried in sugar

Quebec and Boston, two cities where visitors can't understand the locals, now one city where the locals can't understand the locals. The inevitable French–New England patois of the clashing tongues would inject fresh DNA into the stilted Northeast vernacular, producing such sweet, nasally phrases as "pahk le cah dans Hahvahd Yahd." What could be more sing-songy than a redneck Frenchman with a Cambridge accent?

(In technical language, a spontaneous pidgin hybrid would emerge from combining the largely feminine

"capital dialect" of Quebec French with the overt mascu-
linity of non-rhotic Boston English. In layman's terms,
Noam Chomsky would shoot himself in the face.)

Dalgary

KNOWN FOR: *Convict Coliseum,* a reality show combin-
ing executions and rodeos
BIGGEST IMPORT: Buckle polish
BIGGEST EXPORT: Global warming

The inevitability of the Keystone XL Pipeline connecting the vast, oily Alberta tar sands to the vast, oily average Texan makes this megalopolis a
no-brainer. Dallas is often called the
"Calgary of the South," or the other way
around, we're not really sure, but they
are definitely the "each of each other."

Fortunately, "Big D" and "Big C" are
practically connected already, as the
interstitial states of Oklahoma, Kansas,
Nebraska, Wyoming, and Montana are
little more than places where cars broke
down on their way to one of these two

> **IT'S A PROMISE!**
>
> ☞ Work commutes
> from the suburbs will be
> restricted by your vehi-
> cle's mileage. Bicyclists
> will have unlimited range.
> Humvee owners should
> reserve a parking spot at
> the end of their driveway.

fine cities. Once they are physically connected by the pipeline, Dallas and Calgary will find much in common, from
their Museums of Denim to their comparably small popu-
lations of frightened homosexuals.

New Toronto

LONGEST SEASON: Humidity
OFFICIAL ANIMAL: The purse dog
OFFICIAL SONG: "We Will Rockefeller You"

Toronto has long held itself up as a modern hub of global enterprise and cosmopolitan culture. Once we fuse the "Gateway to Hamilton" with New York City, this attitude will finally be justified.

The most significant change for New Torontonians will be in marrying New York's and Toronto's massive theater districts—already two of the world's largest—into one streamlined operation. To this end, all major stages will show the same play, a work of literary genius that combines each country's most popular musical into a single production: *Cats of Green Gables*. Current Toronto thespian Ian Ronningen will star (in every production) as the Canadian orphan mistakenly adopted by the U.S. Legislature, where he lives out his days watching congressional pussies urinating all over the legal process. (Tickets cover the whole seat, but you'll only need the edge!)

1.5 Understanding Hockey, from the Country That Gave You Football and Basketball

THE CONCEPT of sports as a metaphor for war goes back as far as sports, metaphors, and wars. Early athletic competitions were little more than wars with sidelines. Who can forget the Euphrates Bowl of 632 BCE, when Babylon's Hanging Gardeners routed the Fighting Nebuchadnezzars 26–7? It was from this legendary game that we acquired the tradition of slaves pouring a vat of blood over "Coach Pharaoh's" head in a victory celebration, which of course led to the tradition of slaves being buried alive with their coaches.

As Canadians find actual wars costly and inconvenient, we've become purists in the realm of sports, choosing to honor our athletic forebears by conducting all our murder, rape, and pillaging in controlled sixty-minute sessions on Saturday afternoons. Because we also prize our dry sense of humor, we hold this sport on a sheet of ice, combining the grace of carefree skating with the brutality of beating your colleagues with large wooden sticks. Fights are encouraged. Helmets are worn for show. Teeth are a luxury. We call it "hockey," and it is Canada's theater of war.

> **IT'S A PROMISE!**
>
> ☞ Sports team names must reflect their home cities' civil rights records. Welcome to the NHL, Los Angeles Rodney Kings!

It was hockey—via the Canada-USSR "Friendship Series" in 1972 and the 1980 "Miracle on Ice" between the USSR and the U.S.—that prevented the Cold War from going all nuclear. It is hockey, ironically, that makes Canadians so nice; after just *watching* a game, we are too tired to fight. Even the players—talking to the media after an hour of savagely pummeling the other team with elbows, sticks, pucks, and fists—have nothing but kind words for the opponents they just spent sixty minutes trying to kill. "Yeah, I knew when he pulled the shiv out of his boot and stabbed me in the back of the neck that he wanted the goal. That's dedication, and I really respect that, good on him." Game over. Matter settled. Help me reattach my arm and we'll go get some beers.

Hockey is the great peacemaker, and Canada has been campaigning the United Nations for years to get countries to settle their disputes through hockey games. (It's late in the third period. The Israeli Assassins are down by one

---

🍁 **CANAFACT**

In 1891, Ontario native Dr. James Naismith created "soccerballand2peach-baskets," later simplified to "peachball," "soccerand2," "soccerbasket," "ballandpeach," "ballbasket," "balland2peaches," and finally, "basketball."
A few years later, a Canadian team introduced Americans to a modified version of "rugby football," which the Americans ironically shortened to "football" after taking most of the footy parts out.

....

goal, with the Palestinian Bombers on a power play. The winner takes Jerusalem. Never mind the sheer entertainment value of watching desert countries play an ice sport, the prevalence of low-scoring games prevents either team from dominating, so they would just alternate victories year after year and end up sharing the Holy City after all. Problem solved, and never more than one player beheaded with a skate blade. Now let's go get some beers.)

As the world's predominant hockey country, Canada would be happy to host these games and provide referees with the requisite blue helmets. Imagine the global TV rights and jersey sales. Move over tar sands, Canadaddy has a new cow to milk.

As Americans may only be familiar with hockey through the movie *Slap Shot* and the silver-medal game against Canada in the 2010 Olympics,* we've attempted to explain the sport through references that may be familiar to our southern neighbors.†

---

* Although we refer to it as the "gold-medal game."

† We understand that diabetes affects the eyes, but if you are going to televise our games, we beg you not to add a streaking fireball indicating the puck's location. It hurts our tummies.

The *Very* Basics of Hockey

PERSONNEL
1 goalie + 5 players per team (think 1 coffee + 5 donuts per breakfast)

PLAYING SURFACE
Sheet of ice (think a frozen basketball court)

EQUIPMENT
Puck (think ball)
Stick (think baseball bat or toilet snake)
Helmet (think helmet)

OBJECTIVE
Put puck in the net (think mortar round in cave opening)
Goalie stops puck (think Homeland Security and a brown person)
Score more than opponent (think obvious)

OTHER TERMS
Faceoff/puck drop (think unlocking the mall doors for a Nike shoe debut)
Body checking (think armless football tackles)
Offside (think nailing your neighbor's spouse, in their bed)
Penalty Shot (think "two for flinching")
Roughing (think being an asshole)
Icing (think . . . we actually don't know what this is*)

---

* (Icing is the most subjective call in hockey. If a player shoots the puck down the ice from behind the half, and it travels past the opposing goal line before any player touches it, play is stopped, and a faceoff occurs back in the shooting player's defensive end. A linesman can call off an icing if he feels like it, had a heavy breakfast, recently broke up with his girlfriend, or wants to throw the Vancouver–Dallas game on February 26, 2012.)

LENGTH OF PLAY

Three twenty-minute periods (think ¼ of a baseball game, with twice the beer)

As you may have guessed, we intend to make hockey the official sport of the United States of America. We realize the hobby known as baseball has already claimed the title of "America's pastime," and we agree the past is where it belongs. We're confident that Americans will embrace hockey, especially the fighting—something baseball has tried to implement, but it always looks like ninety blindfolded squirrels chasing a greased nut. Amazingly, nobody ever manages to hit anybody, which is sad, since hand-eye coordination is the only whiff of athleticism baseball requires.

You will enjoy hockey's futuristic, arena-of-death feel, and though baseball fans will have fewer opportunities to nap during games, they will easily relate to hockey fans, who are equally drunk and privileged. Once Americans embrace hockey with the same zeal as they do desperate housewives and bottled water, the sport will be embraced by the world. Imagine the day when a UN Security Council speech concludes with: " . . . and we intend to leave it on the ice, Mr. Secretary General. We'll get 'em next year."

1.6 The Cameron Plan: America in 3D

ONE SPRING day in 1905, Albert Einstein held a wrestling match with the speed of light. Unable to pin down a core assumption of Newtonian physics—that velocities could be added one upon the other without end—Einstein gave up the match and tried to be happy that he had lasted a full three rounds.

Then he recalled a moment he rode a streetcar in Bern, watching a clock tower behind the train recede into the distance. He tried to imagine how the tower would appear if the train were traveling the speed of light, and realized that it would not recede at all, because the light from the tower could not catch up to the speeding vehicle. The clock on the train, however, would continue to tick away. This was his eureka moment that changed human history—the realization that time and distance are not fixed notions, but relative to the observer. Einstein immediately posted this on his Facebook page as "OMG, speed of light constant, time totally not! Relativity much?" People liked it, and suddenly everybody wanted to be his friend.

Einstein's musing about the clock tower is what's known as a "thought experiment," a mental parkour adventure in which one imagines hypothetical scenarios to work through a complex problem. Thought experiments have guided the greatest minds in history to explore dimensions of their fields that are simply unimaginable through conventional testing.

Long before being elected to office, our politicians find themselves on the mat just as Einstein did, wrestling with the one thing in the universe that moves faster than the speed of light—a moral indoctrination by their political party. The candidates don't stand a chance, and their imaginations succumb to a chokehold before the opening bell ceases its echo. This lack of imagination in public office is death for a democracy, as every debate is painted in two dimensions: black or white, liberal or conservative, patriot or terrorist. Our leaders are masters of the long and wide argument, but suffer paralyzing vertigo if asked to plumb the depths of compromise.

Which is why, once elected, we will appoint Canadian director James Cameron to bring a much-needed third dimension to the sinking Titanic that is our political universe. As our Director of Time and Space, Cameron will take control on all issues Congress and the Senate cannot solve within thirty days. He will be given broad powers to steer the conversation onto dimensional planes the parties had never considered possible.

A conversation in a Cameron-led legislature may go something like this:

REPUBLICANS: Abortion bad! Women bad for hurting babies!

DEMOCRATS: Choice good! Men bad for controlling women!

CAMERON: Okay, both of you just shut the fuck up for a minute.

Republicans, you believe life begins at conception, and a woman's right to control her body does not supersede the right of the child to be born. That's a valid point, and I applaud your commitment to the sanctity of what you perceive to be an innocent life, even though you support sending teenagers to the electric chair. But that's another conversation.

Democrats, you believe the fetus is a part of the woman and not a separate entity until it is born, and the government does not have the right to tell you what to do with your body. That's a valid point, and I applaud your commitment to personal liberty, even though you won't acknowledge your opponent's confusion when you reserve your sanctity-of-life speeches for murderers on death row. But that's another conversation.

You might notice that you have named your positions "Pro-Choice" and "Anti-Abortion," rather than "Pro-Abortion" and "Anti-Choice." That should tell you something—you are both in favor of an individual's right to make their own choices, and neither of you want abortion to be so rampant it's offered at concierge desks and drive-through windows. But such shrill and endless debate has cost women their preventive health care and cost us all more than one million abortions a year. You're both losing far more than you're gaining.

So let me offer you a third option. First—and forgive me if I'm repeating myself—shut the fuck up. Second, let's talk to our scientists and see if they can find a way for people to have sex without getting pregnant. Perhaps with a little research we can develop some sort of "control of birth" pill, or something else contrary to conception. I know an F/X guy who's a wiz with this stuff. Let me give him a call.

With a little science and an inexpensive public information campaign, we can take a break from the stalemate and dramatically reduce abortions immediately, then get back to fighting over the moral issue in about a year or so after we've made it a far lesser problem. This will free us up to handle other issues like immigration, where I can help you understand the immigrant's point of view by becoming—forgive me—an alien avatar.

I apologize—I really wanted to direct comedies.

1.7 How to Say You're Sorry without Looking like a Total Pussy

....

THE FOLLOWING is an actual transcript from the March 17, 2009, episode of the Fox News program *Red Eye*, featuring Fox larvae Greg Gutfeld, Doug Benson, Bill Schulz, and Monica Crowley:

GREG GUTFELD: Due to personnel and equipment shortages, Canada's Lieutenant General Andrew Leslie—an unusual name for a man—told the Senate defense committee last week, quote, "We will have to explore the possibility of taking a short operational break, that is synchronized of at least one year." Meaning the Canadian military wants to take a breather, to do some yoga, paint landscapes, run on the beach in gorgeous white Capri pants. Leslie added that there is no one to repair the tanks, nor are there any ready tanks for soldiers to train on, so a hiatus is needed to get their armored act together. Doug, I go to you first, because this is a very important question, I want you to take it seriously. Isn't this the perfect time to invade this ridiculous country? They have no army.

DOUG BENSON: I didn't even know that they were in the war. I thought that's where you go if you don't want to fight, go chill in Canada.

GUTFELD: Exactly! Exactly!

BENSON: So I guess they'll have ... that will be their tourism, that will be their selling point. "We're not in the war for a year. Come on by while we nap!"

GUTFELD: Exactly! It's amazing! I don't know any country that's done this! Phil, would Canada be able to get away with this if they didn't share a border with the most powerful country in the universe?

BILL SCHULZ: No, they probably wouldn't. I mean, does this surprise any of us?

GUTFELD: It surprises me.

SCHULZ: Well, you're stupid. We have police officers, and they have Mounties. Our cops ride heavily armored cars, they ride horses. We have bulletproof vests, they have wonderful little red jackets that can be seen a mile away. This is not a smart culture, Greg.

MONICA CROWLEY: So they're getting manicures, they're getting pedicures, everybody needs a little time off.

GUTFELD: Isn't Canada doing, Monica, what most of Europe does anyway, which is just rely on USA in case anything bad happens?

CROWLEY: Of course, they couldn't take a year off from their military if they didn't have the security backdrop of the United States.

SCHULZ: But the other thing you should be worried about, Greg, is: Canada starts this, who's our other border, Mexico, they're gonna start relying on our army too. Remember, it's not Canada, it's Mexico that likes the siestas. It's happening.

This was, of course, horribly offensive to Canadians, who enjoy a good siesta as much as the next nation-state. The other stuff was pretty bad too, and once the YouTube video was translated into Canadian,* outrage was had. In the passive tense. Because we're Canada.

In short, we asked for an apology, because it turned out Canadian soldiers were dying in Afghanistan at a rate of up to four times that of British and American soldiers. Following thousands of complaints, as well as a demand from the Canadian defense minister, Gutfeld issued an "apology" that included the standard phrase that mother weasels teach their young: "I realize that my words may have been misunderstood."†

So, on behalf of Canada, we'd like to take this opportunity to apologize for misunderstanding you.

See how easy that was? We didn't say, "We apologize that you misunderstood our misunderstanding." We just apologized. Didn't even mean it. Doesn't matter.

IT'S A PROMISE!

☞ Unaccepted apologies will be recycled at the Department of My Bad to encourage sustainable communities.

‖‖‖‖‖‖‖‖‖‖‖‖‖‖‖‖‖‖‖‖‖‖‖‖‖‖‖‖‖‖‖‖‖

If there is one thing Canada can bring to the presidency, a single element of northern culture that can restore America's former reputation as the cowboy with the white hat, it is the concept of humility. Although Canada's best-known exports are cannabis and morally questionable oil, the country dominates the world's apology trade, its citizens issuing more "sorrys" per capita than the next three most docile countries combined.

The most common misunderstanding about apologies is that they weaken your position because it seems,

---

* We really don't understand a lot of your accents.

† There may have been other apologies out there, but we didn't find them. In our defense, we didn't look very hard.

on the surface, that you are admitting you're wrong. But we of the sophisticated atonement are here to tell you that you *are* wrong, whether you are right or wrong. So just be wrong and get it over with. Bam. You have cleared yourself to be a complete douchebag again at a later date. Do you now see the power of the apology? It is a weapon of unimaginable modesty. This is how you conquer.

🍁 CANAFACT

Canada's Radio Act forbids lying on broadcast news. Coincidentally, there are no Fox affiliates in Canada.

We would like to introduce you to the standardized, fill-in-the-blank apology form we issue to our fourth graders to prepare them for a life of being a Canadian. This simple tool will get you started on your journey toward becoming a better, meeker nation. Only then may you inherit the earth.

Dear (injured party),

On (date), I made an ass of myself. I did not misspeak. I was not misunderstood. I was not drinking or on drugs, and even if I were, it would not excuse my behavior.

If I had claimed something was true that wasn't, I have since informed myself and am better for the experience.

If I was insensitive or judgmental, I have put myself in your place and am better for the experience.

If I destroyed your property with vomit or bodily fluids, I will replace the affected items and any beer I drank.*

In any event, I let my pride get the best of me, and I apologize. I am a work-in-progress. Let's go get drunk. My treat.

---

* The legal drinking age in Canada is eight.

Drama complete. No need to explain your intent, no helping people "get the joke," no accusing your audience of being an enabler. Again, this is a child's model. Over time, you will learn to personalize your apologies and craft your own sincerity. An adult apology might look something like this:

Dear Fox viewers and other affected parties,

We, the hosts and guests of the Fox News program *Red Eye*, apologize for the comments on our March 17 program.

We will not blame it on you, the viewer, for misunderstanding us. We were clearly being assholes.

We will not claim we were just doing comedy, as we realize the word "News" is actually in our network's title.

We have done some research, and have discovered the following facts:

· Leslie is a common, gender-neutral name, and in this context a *last* name. We apologize for our immature sexism and for making fun of a decorated veteran of the Afghanistan War, which we started.

· Canada is actually our closest ally, and thus not prime invading material. Further, they hold the tragic distinction of losing the most soldiers per capita of any participating nation in the Afghanistan coalition, and our comments were poorly timed to the deadliest month of the war for Canadian soldiers. We apologize for dishonoring these servicemen, particularly since none of us have served in the military ourselves.

· Despite the fact that their Mounties ride horses and wear red jackets, Canada has one-third the murder rate of the

United States, with less than half the police per capita. We assume this is because they apologize a lot.

· Canadians like siestas.

We are sorry, and better for the experience. We promise that every morning from now on, we will wake up, brush our teeth, look ourselves in the mirror, and say, "Good morning. Don't be a dick today."

Now let's go get drunk. Our treat.

······································ **②**

IT'S A SMALL WORLD
(UNLESS YOU'RE LIECHTENSTEIN)

2.1 American Exceptionalism, or How to Make Other Countries Feel Bad about Their Bodies

A WORD served as comfort food to those who swallow the concept of manifest destiny, "exceptionalism" promotes the idea that the United States is... well... really, really awesome. Not just awesome, but *Empire Strikes Back* awesome, if *Star Wars* was the foundational Greek democracy and *Return of the Jedi* was the expansion of American ideals across the globe.*

It would have been perfect if the doctrine of American exceptionalism had ended there, but its popularity led us to a string of self-indulgent prequels with fabricated storylines that favored sappiness and explosions over

---

* If you haven't seen the *Star Wars* movies, please move on to the next chapter, because it's just going to get worse.

meaningful content. (WMDs in Iraq = *The Phantom Menace,* Fox News = *Attack of the Clones,* and the War on Terror = *Revenge of the Sith.*) Add a little CGI to the digital rerelease of the "reason we invaded Iraq" storyline, and suddenly we believe Jabba the Hutt was running the country, and Iraqi civilians actually start to look like Sand People.

Not that America *isn't* awesome. As your continental BFF, we're here to tell you that you are, in so many ways, for so many reasons. We love the smell of your hair, which is where we live because we are right on top of you. We love the way you look at us across the tar sands, flirty and hungry. We know it's just the oil, but we like to pretend it's . . . a little more. Just look at our terror alert system:

CANADIAN TERROR ALERT SYSTEM

SEVERE
CALL AMERICA.

HIGH
CHARGE TASERS AND
LOAD CANADA'S GUN.

ELEVATED
ASK BRITAIN IF THEY'RE PLAYING
A PRACTICAL JOKE ON US.

GUARDED
PUT ON PANTS IN CASE
TERRORISTS VISIT.

LOW
ENJOY THE SUNSHINE.

The point is, we all know you're the world's quarterback. We all know you won State three years in a row, and speaking for the rest of the team, we're grateful, and even still somewhat impressed. Taiwan still has your picture taped to her locker—seriously, everyone has a crush on you.

So stop milking it. Do you know how it hurts the world's feelings every time you call yourself the "greatest country in the universe" and "God's chosen nation"? How would you like it if aliens beamed down to earth every few days just to remind humans what an inferior species we are? Or if God revealed that he was actually pointing at the country behind you?

♦ CANAFACT

The term "American exceptionalism" was first coined by Joseph Stalin as an insult to the United States (TRUE). Stalin also claimed he could see Canada from his house, but he did not pretend that it counted as foreign policy experience (SHOULD BE TRUE).

The international community once bought into your invincibility, but now when we hear the phrase "American exceptionalism," we focus on the "exception" part, as in, liberty and justice for all, *except* gays, women, minorities, immigrants, whistle-blowers, documentary filmmakers, prisoners, activists, pacifists, atheists, environmentalists, occupiers, soldiers, veterans, the homeless, the uninsured with preexisting conditions, and anyone standing in line at an airport.

In other words, the very people who make you exceptional.

What this really boils down to is a self-esteem issue. It's nothing to be embarrassed about—we all get down on ourselves from time to time and feel like we have to lash out at our friends. Just look at North Korea, so heartbroken by South Korea's rejection that he's spent the past sixty years locked in his room writing creepy stalker hate mail.

You are better than this, America. You *are* exceptional, but there is an important difference between patriotism (loving who you are) and nationalism (hating what is not you). Practicing nationalism under the guise of patriotism is kind of like saying you don't hate homosexuals because they're gay, you hate them because they're not straight.

IT'S A PROMISE!

☞ The creepy cyclopean pyramid on American money will be replaced with a universal symbol of exceptionalism and enterprise: William Shatner, winking.

But there is hope in humility, a genetic variant all Canadians carry, and that we would be happy to share with our new nation-mates. Humility enables us to openly admit our shortcomings and seek ways to better ourselves. It is not the concentration of power that makes a country great, it is the humble use of that power to bring out the greatness in others. America needs to be exceptional where it counts—swooping in on the *Millennium Falcon* to save Luke rather than manning the controls of the Death Star. For America to be great again, it must remember what it means to be good. To paraphrase a certain bun-headed princess, *Help us, America. You're our only hope.*

2.2 Killing with Kindness, Torturing with Tenderness

OVER THE past decade, Western intelligence agencies have replaced actual intelligence-gathering with airport fondling, shoe fetishes, and a snippy demeanor that would make a Frenchman bathe in disgust. Canadian intelligence-gathering techniques can lend a certain passive-aggressive style that American agencies sometimes lack (except, of course, the aggressive part).

To illustrate this point, we propose to revise the CIA interrogation manual to reflect a more modern approach and helpful attitude.

Introduction to the CIA Interrogation Manual

Revision: July 4, 2013

Welcome to the exciting world of torture! The United States has a rich and noble history of promoting "enhanced cooperation" from our enemies. From the Boston Knee-Cap Party of the American Revolution to the Tokyo Titty Twister of World War II, the U.S. has always been on the forefront of information-gathering techniques. You are now a part of this great tradition, and due to recent developments on the world stage (thank you, Al Qaeda!), you have more weapons at your disposal than ever before. We know you're eager to begin your journey, so let's review our most recent torture updates.

The modern enemy combatant is more educated and worldly than his predecessors, and this manual includes new interrogation techniques to keep pace with the sophisticated terrorist. For example, while there is always

🍁 CANAFACT

Canadian spies cloak themselves in politeness so as not to be mistaken for American spies.

....

room for a classic like bamboo shoots under the fingernails, it's equally agonizing to force prisoners to watch YouTube videos with a 56k dial-up connection. You can also weaken the resistance of detainees by overloading their Facebook status posts—frequent updates on the weather and the consistency of the bean salad you're having for lunch are particularly grating on the nerves, and can produce valuable information from your captive.

Our recent operations in Guantanamo Bay have been productive in introducing a line of fresh, excruciating torments, such as forcing captives to watch countless reruns of *Friends,* edited to include only scenes relevant to the romance between Ross and Rachel. Terrorists who have lived among Westerners for an extended period of time may prove resistant to this technique, in which case we recommend withholding the final episode so they won't know how everything turned out for the couple. Alternatively, you can force your prisoner to watch the entire first season of *Dexter,* but with all of Dexter's parts edited out, leaving behind only hammy overacting from two-dimensional ancillary characters.

Should your secret detention facility be located in a low-tech environment, such as Chechnya, Baghdad, or Alabama, more primitive techniques might be called for. Nothing gets under the well-read terrorist's skin more than bad punctuation, so in the absence of digital (i.e., spell-checked) torture techniques, try planting errors in your prisoner's forced confession. Research has shown that misplaced apostrophes especially weaken resistance, so instead of sentences like "I was the architect of the bombings at your World Trade Center," try "I was the architect of the bombing's at you're World Trade Center."

A more potent version of this technique involves utilizing the contracted form ("it's") when the possessive form ("its") is called for. For example, instead of "I am dedicated to the annihilation of the Zionist state and all its infidel supporters," try "I am dedicated to the annihilation of the Zionist state and all it's infidel supporters."

Lastly, while everyone loves a good waterboarding, the sophisticated terrorist has trained against this technique, so more drastic measures might be called for. We recommend forgoing the boutique labels (such as Idaho Ice and Essentia) and waterboarding with a selection from our list of more pedestrian brands, including Dasani, Aquafina, and Poland Spring. If your detainee is suspected of environmental terrorism, it is particularly effective to waterboard with a brand that carries a heavy carbon footprint—Aqua Fiji, for instance—and then throw the empties right into the garbage. For the direst of situations, when information is crucial to prevent an imminent attack, our legal advisors have approved the use of tap water. (Please note, however, that the Geneva Convention prohibits using water drawn from aquifers in New Jersey.)

> **IT'S A PROMISE!**
>
> ☞ Guantanamo Bay will be closed and the prisoners moved to the arctic, where they can be legally snowboarded.

2.3 Weaponizing Politeness: Fight like a Canadian!

WE KNOW how much Americans like war. Who wouldn't? Rockets' red glare, bombs bursting in air, all that jazz. And when there are no wars to be had, there are always metaphorical wars to fall back on, like the War on Drugs and the War on Terrorism.

Sure, they're not as sexy as real wars, but at least they are never designed with an endgame in mind—declaring "war" on something allows a country to commit unlimited resources for unspecified political purposes for an indefinite amount of time without having to worry about little things such as principles or facts. It's like the Fox News research department on a national scale.*

IT'S A PROMISE!

☞ Every declaration of war, no matter how small, will include a partial draft to hold citizens accountable for the officials they elect. Video gamers will be the first to go, since they are already trained and have nothing better to do.

Don't get us wrong—Canada is always up for a good scrap when the situation warrants, and as America's pinkie buddy, we've got your back. We paved the way for you in World Wars I and II. We smuggled the American diplomats out of Iran during the 1980 hostage crisis. Even now we are backing the U.S. effort in Afghanistan, suffering our highest number of casualties since the Korean War. And rest assured, should the terrorists ever declare a jihad on the Baconator or the McRib, we will lounge with you, side by side, defending the salted meat-substitutes of freedom.

But do you know what we really like in Canada? Syrup. And peace. We are *totally* into the peace thing up here. We know it's not sexy, but it is cheap. And peaceful.

Canada has gotten far more mileage out of peace than out of war. Our humanitarian and negotiation efforts during the Vietnam and Cold Wars saved countless lives and helped bring about resolution to both conflicts. Our "Operation Yellow Ribbon" on 9/11 welcomed 33,000

---

* We're kidding, of course. Everyone knows Fox News doesn't have a research department.

passengers in more than 220 airplanes diverted from U.S. airspace, our communities opening their doors to feed and shelter Americans until they could return home. The very concept of "peacekeeping" was invented by future Canadian prime minister Lester B. Pearson to bring about an end to the 1956 Suez Crisis, earning him the Nobel Peace Prize (and, we're guessing, no small amount of cred with the ladies).

As your president, we will bring to a battle-weary America a notion of peace as something other than "the brief moments that happen between wars." Or, to borrow the metaphor one more time: once elected, we will declare War on War.

War is an after-the-fact expenditure, meaning we go to war only because we failed to address the conditions (poverty, bigotry, ignorance, and greed) that bring it about. If we had seriously addressed global warming in the 1980s when we started pretending we cared about it, it would be a minor issue now. If we brush and floss like our dentists tell us to do, we won't have cavities later. And that is our plan for America—instead of a dental drill, America will be the world's fluoride, preventing economic and social decay in those hard-to-reach places.

War is so 1940s, '50s, '60s, '70s, '90s, and 2000s. If the level of funding that America has wasted on the less focused wars (about $2 trillion over the past ten years) had instead been invested in human potential, the root causes of war would be largely obliterated, and our soldiers would now be refereeing Lincoln-Douglas debates in Libyan high schools and sculpting sand art for a thriving ecotourism industry in Yemen.

As America's commander-in-chief, we would also take advantage of underutilized weapons in the American arsenal—the entertainment and technology industries, for instance. America has effectively used public-private partnerships in the past to address domestic issues. Imagine if we used them on an international scale. North Korea wants to conduct nuclear tests? *Bam!* We bench Kobe Bryant until Kim Jong-un relents. India decides to invade Pakistan? *Bam!* Microsoft cripples the Bangalore economy by recalling its tech-support staff.

We understand our efforts will fall short of achieving world peace, but perfection is not something to be achieved, it is something to be aimed for. If nothing else, the public-relations benefit from repurposing the world's most dominant military—redefining its primary mission as building things rather than blowing them up—is nearly incalculable. Winning wars is costly and bloody. Winning hearts and minds is cheap and effective. In no time, protestors will stop burning American flags and start burning DVDs of the *Star Trek: Enterprise* series, as nature intended.

✤ CANAFACT

We gave you Shatner. You gave us Bakula. (Who? Exactly. Do the math.)

Within a few short months, the U.S. is back in style. Pro-American hashtags like #TehranlovesUSA and #chubforAmerica will resonate through cyberspace. The world will return to its doe-eyed admiration for everything American: jeans made in Vietnam, iPhones assembled in China, apple pies made with fresh Mexican apples and picked by fresh Mexican immigrants. Eventually, the metaphorical use of "War" will change as well, and the Wars on Drugs and Terrorism will be rightfully prosecuted as Wars on Poverty and Ignorance.

It's impractical to assume every petty tyrant will climb right on board the peace train, as many of them seem to enjoy slapping around their own people when they can't find a smaller country to pick on. When governments attack their own citizens, the United Nations usually responds with warnings that the country will be warned, again and again, the way your dad warned you he'd pull the car over if you didn't stop screwing around in the back seat, but he never did, and that was the day you learned the meaning of the phrase "empty threat." To bypass this toothless process, we have created a template letter that will be issued to the offending government once—and only once.

Dear (leaders of offending country),

Please stop attacking your citizens, even though all the (shooting/grenading/bombing/tanking/raping) makes our democracy look pretty damn good in comparison. We understand your lack of (nuclear weapons/fresh water/ Victoria's Secret outlet stores) makes you feel inferior to other nations, but punching yourself in the face doesn't make the other people in the room less attractive.

We would prefer not to bomb your home at (address) because we honestly don't have a (security/economic/new Disney park) interest in your country right now. Please remember that it is an election year, and war (does/does not) seem to be trending favorably at the moment.

However, since we are suddenly taking heat from our (country of origin)-American community, we need to at least look like we are doing something. Hence, we have set up a committee to look into the situation, which should buy you the time you need to solve this crisis on your own before we send FedEx Seal Team 6 to your (palace/summer retreat/"secret" bunker at coordinates 40.762469, 73.974155).

We respectfully request you stop being a douchebag to your own citizens. Immediately. Our oil mappers are already hard at work.

Kind Regards,

President Canada

2.4 Showing Nature Who's Boss

HUMAN BEINGS exist in a gaseous state—we expand to fill the space we're allowed. Give us an ocean, and we'll build boats. Give us gravity, and we'll build rocket ships. Give us purple mountain majesties and amber waves of grain, and we will cover every square inch of it with billboards promoting "Purple-Mountain Souvenirs" and "World's Amberest Grain Kernel." If global warming hadn't come around, global elbowing would have eventually wiped us out anyway.

You know what else has elbows? Polar bears. How do we know? Because we see them rotate out of the water every time they take a breaststroke across what used to be a glacier field but is now a summer pond.

The good news is, Americans are not without a proud history of genuine conservation efforts. In 1916, U.S. president Woodrow Wilson founded the National Park Service, a decision that would one day draw millions of travelers from around the world to the Grand Canyon Visitor Center, where they would watch *Grand Canyon: The Movie* in pants-pooping IMAX, and then go home without bothering to see the actual Grand Canyon, which is only seven miles away.

Nearly a century of environmental awareness later, the world's five largest oil companies have raked in more than a trillion dollars in profit in the last decade alone, while enjoying $22 billion in U.S. government subsidies to support the private jets and country estates that have proved vital to stopping international terrorists, which of course are just polar bears with exploding backpacks strapped to their elbows.

 CANAFACT

Canada is home to the famous "Maple Sands," where, due to increased demand for syrup, engineers frack the soil beneath maple groves to collect and bottle hidden residue. Two tons of soil = one jar of syrup. Tap, baby, tap!

We of the vast, untamed northern wilderness share with our southern neighbors this fondness for pretending we give a shit about the planet. We realize that environmentalism is more a fashion statement than a devotion to actual change, but to make the fashion an actual "statement," there needs to be a certain level of commitment, and we fear that we are just not pretending hard enough.

Take, for instance, our tendency to judge a creature's right to live based on some twisted Darwinian notion of "survival of the cutest." We might throw ourselves in front of a bullet to protect a baby seal, like the arctic secret service, but we don't think twice about ordering a chicken nugget that was born and raised in the animal equivalent of Auschwitz, fattened on arsenic and animal waste, then ushered into the sweet release of death to become the meatlike half of a bite-sized morsel. If baby seals were as ugly and tasty as chicken, they would appear on lobster bibs instead of the cover of *National Geographic*.

IT'S A PROMISE!

☞ **We will continue building oil pipelines, but they will carry maple syrup. If there's a spill, at least the animals will be tasty.**

This commitment to simulated environmentalism also includes hunting, an activity that makes eco-narcissists swoon in faux disgust.* But let's face it—no wild animals die of boredom after a long retirement. If you were an old deer with a great rack, and someone offered you the option to die quickly and be made into a statue instead of being eaten alive by a predator, wouldn't you jump at that? Well, you wouldn't jump, because you're old and supporting a huge rack, but after you were shot and stuffed, they'd probably make you look like you were jumping.

As your democratically elected leader, Canada is committed to pretending to care about the environment just enough so your grandchildren can play outside without donning a beekeeper's outfit and an inch-thick coating of SPF 90. The world is equally doomed either way, but if we're going to play pretend, let's not phone it in—let's wear the costumes and learn the dialogue to make the play as enjoyable as possible.

Therefore, in the hopes of winning a Tony for Best Scenic Design, we will replace the numbers on gas pumps

---

* We strongly endorse the fashion sense of the good people of Dawson City, Yukon Territory, for what seems to be a mandatory "wear what you kill" policy.

with images of hidden costs, like trees and polar bears and little Timmy's carcinoma. If you're going to spend green at the pump, you should see what kind of greenery you are actually spending. Instead of numbers flipping by, there will be pictures of salmon and whales and melting glaciers. Instead of figuring out it will take twenty bucks to drive from Tulsa to Dallas, you'll see it will cost eight oil-slicked seagulls and a wolf with a speech impediment. Instead of telling the attendant to "top it up," you'll say, "throw a humpback in the tank!"

To maintain the spirit of keeping up appearances, all members of our administration will be required to demonstrate they know the difference between "climate change" and "the weather." We will close all highways that do not carve a straight line from City A to City B, returning nature to ... well, nature. If you are too lazy to get out of your car to see a deer, then you do not deserve to see a deer. So-called "scenic" highways will be dismantled, as there are so many Starbucks that the grizzly bears have become jittery and started writing novels. It kind of takes the adventure out of it when you can drive through the hinterland of Yellowstone and the only wildlife you see is Gentle Ben foraging for dark mochas and free wireless.

🍁 **CANAFACT**

In 1970, a group of concerned Canadians created the "Don't Make a Wave Committee." Later realizing that it is the actual making of the wave that disturbs the surface-quo, they renamed the group "Greenpeace."

A key feature of our environmental platform will be combating that most lazy of false practices linking the human and natural worlds: the anthropomorphizing of animals. Specifically, people who put hats on dogs.

Our solution: quit putting hats on dogs. No doubt humans share basic feelings with our friends in the animal kingdom—love, fear, joy, anxiety, and the occasional overwhelming desire to poop on our neighbor's lawn. But do we really want to imbue our pets with a fashion sense? Does it further our species to treat other species as "people accessories"? It's no wonder third-world countries don't like us—our animals are dressed better than they are.

Animals dressed as people are the canary in the coal mine of Western civilization, where the chasm between the needs of our most desperate citizens and the extravagances of our leisure class has become irreconcilably vast. The more frightened we are by our own impending doom, the more we recede into the sanctuary of wheel rims, hair extensions, and little sailor outfits for dogs that we have spent centuries breeding to look like actual sailors. Everyone knows the fall of the Roman Empire was brought about by an increasingly soft lifestyle, an apathy toward worldly problems, and old ladies who made their sheep wear berets. We're pretty sure that at the very end, the caretakers at the Coliseum were knitting toques for their lions.

We don't need scientists screaming from the rooftops about global warming to see that we are a generation away from living in caves and fighting over pictures of food. We just need to glance out the coffee-shop window and see a Chihuahua sporting a yarmulke and matching tartan kilt to know the end of the world is near.

With that in mind, should we (somehow) not achieve the presidency, what follows are some tasty post-apocalyptic recipes for the new Stone Age.

End of Days Brownies

INGREDIENTS

3 soup cans of cocoa-colored exterior house paint

2.5 handfuls of irradiated dirt

2 crushed or grated cockroaches

gravel to taste

INSTRUCTIONS

Whisk ingredients together and pour into a discarded hubcap. Bake under mushroom cloud for one hour.

Uncle's Famous Rump Roast

INGREDIENTS

1 buttock from an uncle (the other other white meat)

1.5 cupped hands of water

1 handful dry sand

1 bunch cauliflower

toe jam to taste

INSTRUCTIONS

Place buttock meat on a hot rock or discarded nuclear control rod and apply the sandy dry rub, thoroughly covering entire roast. When the meat begins to sizzle, spritz with water and toe jam. Decoratively arrange cauliflower on serving tray, place meat, and serve. (Do not eat the cauliflower. It is disgusting.)

Buckshot Soup

INGREDIENTS

1 heaping tuna can of double-aught buckshot

3 soup cans of acid rainwater

1 hobo femur

2 handfuls cedar chips, particleboard, or bark (avoid IKEA laminate furniture, as it is toxic)

INSTRUCTIONS
Revisit scene of gasoline riot. Use a magnet to collect buck-shot from the parking lot until the tuna can overflows. Scavenge other ingredients and return to abandoned dwelling. Combine in helmet and boil until the wood bits melt in your mouth. Pairs well with Grandpa's urine.

Soylent Seth Green
INGREDIENTS
1 Seth Green

INSTRUCTIONS
Gather a Seth Green.* Strain through fine wire mesh. Serve in yogurt cup.

2.5 Un-American Idol: How Reality Shows Can Stop Illegal Immigration

AT THE BASE of the Statue of Liberty reads an inscrip-tion every American fourth grader memorizes during the downtime when they are not learning about science and contraception: "Give me your tired, your poor, your hud-dled masses yearning to breathe free..." It's a popular myth that the statue was a "gift" from France, but Euro-peans know it was a clever scheme to channel the world's yawning, penniless huddle-enthusiasts into a distant land with lots of hiding spaces.

---

* Easily located at San Diego Comic-Con or Cylon bunker in Santa Monica.

As America has lately amassed its own inventory of freedom-seekers (gays, Mexicans, atheists, anyone with a vagina), its solution to foreign whining has been to dole out development money to raise third-world standards just enough that the people there can produce twice as many children, who will then grow up hungry, tired, and yearning to breathe free in greater numbers. And here we are.

Not that America's good intentions should go unappreciated. In 2010 alone, USAID (the agency tasked with converting your tax dollars into gruel and mosquito nets) donated $38 billion to 182 countries, ranging from $5 billion for Afghanistan to $83 for Iceland. (That's not 83 billion dollars, it's 83 dollars, which, we assume, went to their struggling "adopt a vowel" program.)

But the issue here is not America's generosity, it is the fundamental misunderstanding of what downtrodden foreigners actually want. Food? Doesn't last. Money? No pockets. Jobs? The daily commute to America is a bitch. Education? What good is that when you probably won't live past twenty-three?

The fact is, oppressed, starving people around the world want exactly what their free and more-than-sated brethren of the West want: to become famous on a reality show. To that end, we propose reassigning all foreign aid to the

> **IT'S A PROMISE!**
>
> ☞ A lottery system will limit the number of U.S. reality TV show licenses. The first will go to a reality show created to televise the lottery.

development of a global reality-television franchise, with each country receiving enough funding to make nightly programs that run year-round. ($38 billion, divided by 182 countries, divided by 365 days, equals more than a half-million dollars per episode, with plenty left over for a lavish annual Christmas special.)

Why complain about U.S. military bases in your backyard when you can tune in to *Keeping Up with the Kazakhstans*? Why burn American flags in the streets when you could be home watching *The Real Hutwives of Mbanza-Ngungu*? Why spend your leisure time shooing insects off your dying infant's face when you can learn the secrets of *The Fly Whisperer*?

But American support won't stop there—what good is a reality show without celebrity cameos? Watch transfixed as Paris Hilton and Nicole Richie parachute into an Ethiopian refugee camp for a special episode of *The Unbearably Simple Life*! See what Adam and Jamie can do with duct tape, a set of jumper cables, and a hypodermic needle in *Aidsbusters*! Laugh for hours (depending on life expectancy) as Deb and Stella give time-outs to African charity embezzlers in *Nanny NGO*!

More than a temporary distraction, these programs need to deliver the same false hope of a better future enjoyed by America's own ever-expanding underclass. And for that, we will turn to the reality show's math-challenged, lotto-playing cousin, the contest show.

Running from the KGB? Audition for *Dancing with the Czars*! Looking for an advantage over your slightly darker, machete-wielding neighbors? Give them a roadblock in *The Amazing Racism*! Seeking a ticket out of an oppressive Middle Eastern theocracy? Study up for *Are You Smarter Than a Woman*!

🍁 **CANAFACT**
The most popular reality show in Canada is *Kate Plus Eight Meters of Snow*.
....

Take a spin on the *Wheel of Misfortune*! Gamble that sandwich on *Meal or No Meal*! Apply those skills you've learned since birth on *Survivor (For Reals)*! Toss that burka in the garbage and strut for your life on *So You Think You Can Dance but You'd Better Not or We'll Stone You in the Public Square*!

Sure, the average person has the same chance "making it" on a reality or contest show as the Boston Bruins have of *legitimately* winning a Stanley Cup, but that is beside the point. This is the essence of the American Dream, now exported to the rest of the world: it doesn't matter that the poor will always be poor, it only matters that people who inherited their money tell them they won't.

2.6 A Simple Solution for Integrating Our Indigenous Peoples

....

JUST KIDDING. We have no idea.

🍁 **CANAFACT**
Seriously, we are stumped on this one.
....

2.7 The Metric System: Exactly Ten Times More Awesome Than Imperial Units

....

GRANTED, THE system of imperial units still used by the United States—though long abandoned by the rest of the industrialized world—has given us a rich vocabulary of clichés and dead metaphors. (One might say that, as the world inches toward globalization, America is shooting itself in the foot by sitting on its perch, stone-faced, chained to its furlongs and miles, in league with no one, not an ounce of unity, ignoring their backyard neighbors by the pound for reasons we can't fathom.)

Americans like to measure things with their gut. A precise, base-10 system of measurement is a threat to their God-given right to guesstimate. Of course, imperial units are also exact, but their proportions are asymmetrical to the point of being haphazard, sort of a weights-and-measures equivalent to Steve Martin's script choices (1 *Roxanne* = 16 *Bringing Down the House*s = 144 *Pink Panther* remakes).*

It is not as if Americans are unaware of the metric system—modern imperial units are even calculated in terms of metric equivalents. But there is something just a bit too *European* about everybody coming together and agreeing on a standard for anything. Voters put more stock in independent thought than simple math, which is why the economic plans of "outsider" presidential candidates use numbers that don't even remotely add up.

🍁 **CANAFACT**

To make comparison graphics easier to calculate, Canada carefully maintains one-tenth the population of the United States.

....

To assist Americans with the conversion to the metric system—and it is going to happen—we will introduce base-10 units of measurement using elements of popular culture with which they are already familiar. For example:

Ego Mass: 1 O'Reilly = 10 Cowells

Greed Units: 1 BP = 10 Morgan Stanleys

---

* Steve, if you're reading this, do we have a screenplay for you. Seriously. Not even kidding. Call us. 604-254-7191.

Pundit Volume: 1 Limbaugh = 10 Maddows = 100 Mahers

Stage Power: 1 Streep = 10 Dinklages = 100 Sheen Srs. = 1000 Sheen Jrs.

Additionally, we will introduce new units of measurement to keep pace with our rapidly changing culture:

The Palin Second: A measurement of "media whore time," a Palin is the amount of idiocy one is willing to publicly display to get on television for one second. (1000 milli-Palins = 1 Palin = .001 kiloPalins.)

The Lohan Interval: The length of time between escaping one self-imposed disaster and inducing another. (1000 milliLohans = 1 Lohan = .001 kiloLohans.)

The Pitt Ratio: One Pitt indicates an equal proportion of "Looks-to-Talent." A larger Pitt number indicates handsome but inept; a smaller number indicates talented but disfigured. (1000 milliPitts = 1 Pitt = .001 kiloPitts.)

The Romney Mile: The distance of rhetorical digression one is willing to travel before failing to make one's point. (1000 milliRomneys = 1 Romney = .001 kiloRomneys.)

IT'S A PROMISE!

☞ The Supreme Court will be increased to ten members, and their decisions enforced in direct correlation to the vote percentage. Assuming we add one more conservative, corporations will become three-fifths of a person.

The Geraldo Nano: The amount of time elapsed between one's appearance on a talk show and reappearance in a police mug shot. (1000 milliGeraldos = 1 Geraldo = .001 kiloGeraldos.)

The Daily Show Correspondent Hour: The interval between the conclusion of the interview and the moment you realize that you probably shouldn't have agreed to an interview. (1000 milliDailys = 1 Daily = .001 kiloDailys.)

The Colbert Minute: The four minutes of bong hits that follow *The Daily Show*. (1000 milliColberts = 1 Colbert = .001 kiloColberts.)

The Michael Mooremosphere: The proportion of a story someone is not telling you because it conflicts with their agenda. (1000 milliMooremospheres = 1 Mooremosphere = .001 kiloMooremospheres.)

The Cheney Acre: The square footage of influence an individual requires to carry out the devil's bidding. (1000 milliCheneys = 1 Cheney = .001 kiloCheneys.)

The Nancy Gracibel: The exact amount of shrill judgment required to make a television camera involuntarily turn your direction. (1000 milliGracibels = 1 Gracibel = .001 kiloGracibels.)

The Jolie: The volume of sex appeal generated by one straight woman to make other straight women want to make out with her. (1000 milliJolies = 1 Jolie = .001 kiloJolies.)

The Santorawatt: The amount of intellectual energy sucked out of the universe each time Rick Santorum opens his mouth. (1000 milliSantorawatts = 1 Santorawatt = .001 kiloSantorawatts.)

The Shatner: A simple measurement of how cool a Canadian is. (1000 milliShatners = 1 Shatner = .001 kiloShatners.) (Also a measurement of how hard one has been kicked in the testicles, for some reason.)*

---

* Stolen from *The Battle of Burgledorf*. Demand it in your theaters now.

.... **3**

THE IRONY OF
BEING IRONIC IN A
POST-IRONIC AGE

3.1 The Elitist Scourge: How to Hate People Who Are Better Than You

....

A WORD has recently crept into the American political lexicon. A power word. A fine, reliable word with a strong chin and the scent of destiny. A word once clean, but excreted from the mouths of politicians it has become an insult hurled at smart people the way swine might throw pearls . . . at farmers . . . or something like that.

The word is "elite," and it has recently replaced "Nazi" as the favored term of endearment in the Great American Smear-Off. We are waiting for someone to just throw up an attack ad claiming their opponent is "too smart to lead." Some parties (you know who you are) have turned "elite" into a dirty word, making a vice of education* and a virtue

---

* It was on February 25, 2012, that U.S. senator Rick "Home School" Santorum accused President Obama of being a snob for wanting to give every American the opportunity to attend college. We don't have a joke here, we just want to remind everyone how elite Rick Santorum is not.

of ignorance, as if they have simply conceded their queen and decided they are going to try to win with their pawns. (Tea Party Translation: they have foregone the ladders and are trying to win with the chutes.)

The sad truth is, we like idiots in office. Why? Because we want to be able to identify with our leaders. We are so insecure that we need to feel at least as worthy as the very people who, by definition, should be the best we have to offer. Other professions require years of study and exams. Even a driver's license requires proof of vision. All a politician has to do is have the same last name as his well-connected daddy before he drops by the White House to pick up the keys to the invasion-mobile.

> **IT'S A PROMISE!**
>
> ☞ Evolution and creationism will be classified in schools according to their own methodology—the former as a science, the latter as an elective.

We cannot allow our rulers to do to this continent what Madonna did to "American Pie."* This is why we will require all federally elected officials—congressmen, senators, and even future presidents—to pass an exam before their names can be put on the ballot. Think of it as SATs for politicians, but with less Red Bull and more Metamucil.

Sample questions might include:

· Which Korea is our ally?

· Is Africa a country or a continent?

· Whom did Paul Revere warn that the British were coming— the Americans or the British?

---

* She raped it, and she wasn't gentle.

- Does the U.S. government have a "Department of Law"?

- Are New York and Los Angeles part of America?

- Does the United States share a border with Afghanistan?

- Can you name a single Supreme Court decision other than Roe v. Wade?

- What is the difference between "nuclear" and "nucular"?

- How many Iraqis were involved in the September 11 attacks?

- Were environmentalists responsible for the BP oil spill?

- What does the vice president do?

If these questions sound familiar, it's because they are directly lifted from remarks made over the past four years by perennial toddler-in-a-tiara Sarah Palin, who, despite being one Biden-gaffe away from the vice presidency in 2008, would have scored a zero on this test. If this has been an educational experience for you, you may be the first person in history to utter the phrase, "I learned something from Sarah Palin."

It is our hope that this new testing program will quell the deluge of soccer moms, drinking buddies, and V-neck sweater hobbyists flooding the halls of the world's most revered political establishments. No more politicians who think global warming is a conspiracy hatched by polar bears and funded by Al Qaeda. No more elected officials who won't give money to the arts unless it means more

🍁 **CANAFACT**
Sarah Palin is not—we repeat, *not*—from Canada. Let's be very clear about that.
....

Girls Gone Wild videos. No more leaders who look at sand and say, "Hey, I wonder if my car could run on that?"

Until such time that we can enact our pre-candidate exam policy, we ask that American citizens take the concept to heart and seek out informed, educated public servants who are dedicated to reasonable governance rather than enforcing their own armchair ideologies. If this is too much to ask, then at a minimum, the next time you accidentally stab yourself in the teeth with a fork, ask yourself this simple question: "Do I want someone as stupid as me running the country?"

3.2 Citizens Divided: People Are Now Corporations

THERE HAS been much to-do* about the Citizens United decision by the U.S. Supreme Court, poorly but pithily summarized by the chilling line you might expect to find in a dystopian Charlton Heston film: "Corporations are people." It's a complicated legal decision, but essentially Citizens United allows businesses to stop putting politicians on layaway at the Congressman Outlet store, and start purchasing them outright at the Bed, Bath, and Beyond Integrity around the corner.

♦ CANAFACT
Exxon and WalMart are now the largest people in the United States. But the average American is catching up.

The unforeseen side effect of turning more than 30 million businesses into people overnight is the sudden 10 percent increase in the U.S. population, a citizenry already reeling from high unemployment and increasingly scarce

* Yes, in Canada we use phrases like "much to-do," and after we are elected, so will you.

resources. Who will care for these new humans? Do small businesses now have the legal protection enjoyed by dwarves? Can Abercrombie and Fitch legally wed? Who will defend Target from the NRA?

As such challenges cannot be met by the current infrastructure, we have no choice but to reduce the number of actual human face-havers by officially declaring a portion of them to be corporations. In cooperation with the Henderson family of Albany, New York, we have already begun a test program to help Mrs. Henderson transition her economically unfeasible "loving" household into a streamlined model of genetic efficiency.

Memo

To: Members of the Henderson family
From: Mom
Subject: Cutbacks

In light of the current financial situation, it is my sad duty to inform you that we will be downsizing the family in the hopes of remaining a competitive household. Please note that we regard each and every one of you as a valuable member of our organization. However, we are unable to retain a full staff in this troubled economic climate. Jenny, we wish you the best of luck finding a middle-child position in another family that can use your unique qualifications.

In addition to the new layoff policy, the rest of us will have to make sacrifices in order to remain a solvent kinship. Effective immediately, we are instituting a freeze on allowance hikes, bonuses for good grades, and perks such as lunchbox pudding. All travel expenses, including soccer practice and trips to the mall, will be reviewed for cost-effectiveness. Wherever possible, other expenses—such as the twenty dollars Todd gets for mowing the lawn—will be outsourced to the less fortunate Baxter children, who offer better rates with minimal decline in quality.

Since Rebecca is an infant, and thus incapable of independent mastication, she will receive special dispensation from the new "Cutting-Your-Meat-for-You Tax." In a related policy, there will be no more meat. Casual Saturdays will now be even more casual; by making it "underwear only" day, we hope to cut our clothing expenses by one-seventh. The annual family vacation will be held semi-annually in the playroom, which will be shuttered the rest of the year. The backyard swing set will now be operated on a "pay to play" basis. The Christmas present will be shared by all.

Until the economic situation improves, each child will be limited to three prayers to Grandma per week, and no more than two minutes per prayer. All requests for Grandma to "look over" family, friends, and pets must be approved by management. In addition, no family members may have any further contact with Uncle Bob. This policy has nothing to do with the downsizing.

It is incumbent upon each child to bring the spirit of these new measures to bear on their daily decisions in an effort to curb wastefulness and improve efficiency. For example, if you are not tired during nap time, you might find it a nice, peaceful hour to sew wallets. School days might be more fun if you think of "Show and Tell" as "Appraise and Acquire."

In the spirit of parity, management will be making cuts of their own. Daddy will no longer use the joint credit card to buy expensive jewelry for executives that are not Mommy. This will enable Mommy to make fewer investments at the "drinky store," which, in the long run, will save us the expense of acquiring a fourth Daddy. Accordingly, executive compensation packages will be limited to continuing our weekly sessions with Dr. Peterson, who has been working as an outside consultant to keep the organization afloat.

IT'S A PROMISE!

☞ Corporations will still be people, but if they can't provide a birth certificate they will be legally obligated to care for your lawn.

We are certain everyone will work as a team to return the Henderson household to its previous state of fiscal stability. Should you have any ideas you would like to contribute, the suggestion box is in the kitchen (please note the new coin slot).

3.3 **Thoughts on Relieving America's Sexual Tension**

LET'S CUT right to the chase. If God didn't want us fucking like rabbits, He would have designed us for asexual reproduction, like the frigid but numerous amoeba. If God wanted sex reserved for procreation, an orgasm would feel less like heaven and more like acute gastroenteritis. If God didn't want us to know and love our own bodies, He wouldn't have left us with the instructions, "Do unto yourself as you would have others do unto you." (The Word of God is much hotter in the biblical Aramaic.)

Were these divine oversights? No. Did He suffer from some sort of Almighty schizophrenia? No. Was He distracted by Eve's revealing fig bodice? Probably. Because the bottom line is this: God. Loves. Sex. We don't know if He loves having it Himself, but He clearly loves it for His creations. And not just sex, but . . .

Nudity: "At the same time spake the LORD by Isaiah the son of Amoz, saying, Go and loose the sackcloth from off thy loins, and put off thy shoe from thy foot. And he did so, walking naked and barefoot." (Isaiah 20:2)

Exhibitionism: "How glorious was the king of Israel to day, who uncovered himself to day in the eyes of the handmaids of his servants, as one of the vain fellows shamelessly uncovereth himself!" (II Samuel 6:20)

Incest: "And Cain knew his wife; and she conceived, and bare Enoch." (Genesis 4:17) (The only woman on earth at the time was Cain's mom. Ew.)

Fecophilia: "And thou shalt eat it as barley cakes, and thou shalt bake it with dung that cometh out of man, in their sight." (Ezekiel 4:12)

IT'S A PROMISE!

☞ Abstinence-only politicians caught in sex scandals will have to play themselves in the made-for-TV movie.

||||||||||||||||||||||||||||||||||||||||||

Strip clubs: "Behold, I am against thee, saith the LORD of hosts; and I will discover thy skirts upon thy face, and I will shew the nations thy nakedness, and the kingdoms thy shame." (Nahum 3:5)

Penthouse Forum letters: "For she doted upon their paramours, whose flesh is as the flesh of asses, and whose issue is like the issue of horses." (Ezekiel 23:20)

And what the hell, while we're at it, why not:

Fart jokes: "Wherefore my bowels shall sound like an harp for Moab, and mine inward parts for Kirharesh." (Isaiah 16:11)

In fact, God so loves the sexual human that a man can't get any heavenly respect without a working penis: "He that is wounded in the stones, or hath his privy member cut off, shall not enter into the congregation of the LORD." (Deuteronomy 23:1)

And keep in mind, this is just the King James Bible, which—thanks to centuries of papal councils composed of old men who weren't getting any (see "Congressional Hearings on Contraception")—has sanitized the Word of God for your protection. If many of the original books were still included, today's Bible would read less like Bill Clinton's official correspondence and more like Bill Clinton's private diaries.

🍁 CANAFACT

Canadians don't feel shame, because it's too cold to take our clothes off.

The subject here is shame—shame of our bodies, shame of our healthy desires, shame of love—an artificial, unnatural shame used as a weapon against common sense, biological blueprints, and God's own design.

We're quite confident that God, were He to pop down for an official state visit, could author a long list of things human beings should be ashamed of: racism, HMOs, child soldiers, irresponsible stewardship of our natural resources, enough gold plating on Donald Trump's plane to literally support an African orphanage.*

One might notice that "the human body" is not listed on God's "Shame Sheet." And if you believe—as many Americans and Canadians do—in the efficacy of prayer, you

---

* Google "Trump plane." Have an air-sickness bag handy.

must logically conclude that God approves of North America's multi-billion-dollar porn industry. If God wanted to destroy porn, He would drop a divine handful of tornadoes on the Vegas Gomorrah instead of the righteous Midwest, where He kills hundreds of His good and righteous children every year because, according to His vice president of public relations, Pat Robertson, the people just aren't praying hard enough for Him to stop.

The depth and breadth of our obsession with curtailing our natural functions reaches far beyond the belief that gay marriage will bring about the end of the world. Consider the policies of the Federal Communications Commission, an organization that allows unspeakable violence during prime children's viewing hours but imposes fines and revokes licenses for the most innocuous of naughty words. Take, for instance, the policy of not allowing network television audiences to hear the abominable word "asshole." You may hear "ass," and you may hear "hole," but not the two together. Worse, when a program does use the word "asshole," it is the "hole" part that gets bleeped.

Our policy regarding the sensitivities of the broadcast populace is simple. Upon taking office, we will combine all censoring organizations—including the FCC, the MPAA, and the PMRC—into a single federal agency. The primary function of this new agency will be to call every parent in America every night and ask them, "Do you know what your children are watching/listening to/doing right now?" Based on a literal interpretation of the Bible, we believe God would appreciate the sort of personal-responsibility approach to censorship He had in mind when He wrote the Constitution. If He objects to this plan, well... He knows where to find us.

3.4 **The Question of: a) Education**
....

A COMPLETELY fictional—and yet still shocking—Canada Party survey shows nearly half of American teenagers report their future occupation as "being rich." Unfortunately, a career as a millionaire is available to only 1 percent of U.S. citizens, proving that nearly half of America's teenagers lack the math skills to make their dream come true.

Less fictional—and more shocking—are the actual numbers that bear this out. Despite being home to some of the world's best universities, the U.S. has an education deficit that it can barely comprehend because, well, it has an education deficit. With math and science rankings in the mid-twenties internationally, and a literacy rate below most of Eastern Europe, it would not be surprising to learn that most American teens believe the man who created the Dewey Decimal system was actually named "Dewey Decimal."

The Department of Education estimates that the average American reads at an eighth-grade level, and only 15 percent of Americans are "fully literate," meaning, at best, our pop-up version of this book will outsell this edition seven to one. Hey, we get it—learnin' is hard. Numbers can add up to all sorts of things, and if you separate the letters in a word, they can be reassembled to spell an entirely *different* word. How is anybody supposed to concentrate with that kind of inconsistency?

Fortunately, the answer to America's education woes has been sitting just seventy miles off its coast all along. America needs to get right with Cuba.

Canadians find it odd that American politicians are obsessed with getting Israel and Palestine to bump fists on the other side of the world and yet have not been able to resolve a much less holy war within paddling distance. If you believe in peace in the Middle East, certainly there can be peace in the Middle Caribbean. You can bet if Cuba's oil resources were as plentiful as their nickel ore, either their communist ties and human-rights abuses would be summarily ignored or the American flag would be knitting itself another star.

But for educational solutions, it's hard to beat their class-size maximums of twenty-five, school meal programs, before- and after-school care, free tuition, access to postsecondary education, and a national literacy rate of 99.9 percent—second in the world behind Georgia. (Yes, we too think it's ironic that the most literate country in the world is called "Georgia.")

❦ CANAFACT

If Canada and Cuba were laid end to end, people would be all, "what did you do that for?"
....

Canada ignored America's trade embargo against Cuba to maintain a warm vacation spot on the east coast that wasn't Florida. Fidel Castro was even one of Pierre Trudeau's* pallbearers. (The growing number of vitamin D deficiencies in Canada during the sixties gave rise to a foreign policy of being friends with people in warm places. While Americans were burning their bras and dodging the draft, Canadians were working on their base tans.)

Capitalizing on this friendship, Canada, in its role as President of the United States, can establish a mutually beneficial relationship with Cuba by outsourcing the entire U.S. Department of Education. With Cuba's

---

* Canada's fifteenth and fifteenth-and-a-half prime minister.

guidance, American education will return to the standards that once made it the envy of the Western world. Admittedly, Cubans lag far behind the U.S. in vital areas such as crib-pimping and teen pregnancy, but as their cribs are among the most environmentally sustainable on earth, and their newborns enjoy an enviable infant mortality rate, these weaknesses can be overlooked. Cuba is a young, hyper-educated, America-thirsty land of promise, and when it comes to education, they have already done the legwork.

By our transferring the entire Department of Education, Cuba will become a scholarly utopia protected by America, from America. Since the Ed's annual budget is more than half the GDP of Cuba, education will become the country's main industry, and the newly wealthy and modernized Cuba will attract America's best and brightest educators for a civic career revamping the education system in a tropical island paradise.

With the highest doctor-to-citizen ratio in the world and a level of universal health care comparable to (wait for it . . .) Canada, Cuba can serve as a model to revamp America's much-maligned health programs, resolving such contentious issues as prenatal health, child nutrition, and frequent-lounger rewards for diabetics. Further, as the world's first and only nation to achieve sustainable development, Cuba can help the Ed train America's next generation of engineers, architects, and energy executives in the wise use and conservation of natural resources.

IT'S A PROMISE!

☞ Public funding of symphonies and sports teams will require recipients to teach music and sports at inner-city schools. Go Fighting Strings!

Students will also benefit from our plan to provide teachers—America's most underappreciated cat herders—some well-deserved rest. First we will transfer Guantanamo detainees to Thule Air Base, near the arctic circle. The questionable history of Gitmo will be waterboarding under the bridge, and we'll see how desert-born terrorists react to snowboarding instead. The detention facilities will be converted into a special holiday resort big enough to provide every teacher in the U.S. an annual vacation, where they will be pampered with sunny beaches, spa treatments, and personal valets whose main function will be to tell them they are doing a good job. The length of these vacations will be directly proportional to the difficulty of the teachers' work. Inner-city teachers will get three weeks every year. The art teacher at New York's Dalton School will be allowed to press her face against the airplane window as it flies over the island.

After their vacations, teachers will return to their schools relaxed, refreshed, and ready to teach children that there is more out there than what's reported on Lady Gaga's Twitter stream. Over time, frigid relations between America and Cuba will be the stuff of History Channel documentaries, as the distance separating former enemies becomes a romantic boat ride across the warm waters of the gulf. (Please note that, due to the recent addition of an oily sheen across the Gulf of Mexico, these "warm waters" may actually be on fire. We recommend you have some water on hand.)

3.5 Health Care: More Than Just a Dental Plan for Hockey Players

AMERICA CAN rightfully brag about the extraordinary advances in medicine it has brought to the modern world. No longer do men have to endure the perceived impotence of a mere three-hour erection when a simple pill can add a fourth. Gone are the days when women had to grow their own breasts. Americans never again need suffer the ignominy of tucking their own tummies, lifting their own faces, and suctioning their own lipo with some well-executed sit-ups.

But referring to "medical sophistication" as "health care" is like painting your car with speed stripes rather than properly tuning the engine. The medical paint job in the U.S. is impressive, but its health care is badly in need of a tune-up. And tires. And a new car.

American citizens spend more of their income on health care than any other country on earth, and medical costs contribute to more than half of the nation's personal bankruptcies. But the nation ranks fiftieth in the world in life expectancy, and its infant-mortality rate trails forty-five other nations. It's true that American medicine is the best on earth, but only if you can afford it.

❦ CANAFACT

In 2004, Canadians voted the "Father of Medicare," Thomas Douglas, the "greatest Canadian of all time." A Canadian circumcision is known as a "Tommy D."

Since Americans place significant value on the freedom to let other people contract preventable illnesses, it would be unfair for our administration to install the Canadian model of universal health care, no matter how envy-of-the-worldish it is. Instead, we will expand your existing, publicly funded Veterans Administration programs and declare all U.S. citizens veterans of class warfare and thus eligible for basic medical guarantees. Just as countries defeated by the United States are still given assistance to build schools and hospitals, those defeated in the class war will have the pleasure of pap smears and prostate exams they otherwise couldn't afford.

Basic and preventive care for America's 313 million veterans will be partially paid for with a flat tax on cosmetic medical procedures, including your -lifts, -plasties, -mentations, -ductions, peels, -hancements, and of course your nonemergency -ectomies. As Americans spend $10 billion per year on cosmetic surgery, a tax of just 20 percent will pay for the annual health costs of 1.6 million children. Your basic male-potency miracle pills rake in several more billion a year, and, taxed at the same rate, could wipe out childhood obesity and gingivitis in one master stroke.

To help those struggling drug companies and plastic surgeons make up for lost revenue (heaven forbid a Pfizer exec can't afford platinum butt implants), we will actively promote their drugs and services with government-sanctioned surgery gift cards. What better way to celebrate Mother's Day than giving Mom a new set of boobs? And what could possibly say "happy sweet sixteen" better than the gift of rhinoplasty?

On holiday weekends, we will roll out our Mobile Aesthetic Surgery Hospitals (MASH) to cruise the strips and boardwalks of Atlantic City, Long Island, and Malibu, providing impulse-buy customers with the professionalism of a clinic and the convenience of pizza delivery. Share a romantic Valentine's weekend with your sweetie, recovering from couples Botox! Show your country that you are as potent as it is with a Fourth of July "Patriot Phalloplasty"!

As if your new, better you won't make you feel better-you enough, all surgeries will include follow-up letters with details on who else was made better by your own betterment. "Congratulations on your new face! You'll be happy to know your $15,000 investment also gave a *lift*—ha ha—to the youngsters at your local orphanage, who are enjoying their new toothbrushes and dinner vegetables. Thank you for shopping with the United States government."

> **IT'S A PROMISE!**
>
> ☞ Terminally ill patients will have the right to end their lives on their own terms. Religious groups opposing this policy have the right to heal said patients.

3.6 Helping Children Determine Their Value as Future Americans

HELLO KIDS! You are lucky enough to have been born into a society that values integrity and hard work over inherited wealth.

Just kidding! LOL! Actually your future status is largely decided by the status of your parents, amended by ancillary factors such as race, gender, geography, immigration status, and the prevailing political party. Some people like to invoke the phrase "class warfare" when determining status. We prefer to think of it as a "class gangbang," in which your value is determined by who is on top. To clarify your future place in the U.S. caste pyramid, please fill out the following questionnaire and calculate your score at the bottom.

How many parents do you have?
a) 0
b) 1
c) 2
d) Including the help?

How big is your house?
a) I have one?
b) Duplex
c) Mansion
d) I have *one*?

What's your favorite game?
a) Hide and seek with the INS
b) Pin the tail on the honky
c) Monopoly
d) Monopoly for reals

What movie most resembles your life?
a) *The Passion of the Christ*
b) *Dazed and Confused*
c) *Brewster's Millions*
d) The George Lucas rerelease of *Brewster's Millions* with CGI billions

What's your favorite electronic toy?
a) A stick
b) Simon
c) Xbox
d) NASDAQ

Who is your personal hero?
a) Che Guevara
b) Malcolm X
c) Harvey Milk
d) Alan Greenspan

How many brown children are in your classroom?
a) Most
b) Some
c) I see the janitor on occasion
d) Do tans count?

IT'S A PROMISE!

☞ We will change the phrase "job creators" to "job creationists," and give them seven days to actually create some.

||||||||||||||||||||||||||||||||||||||||||||||||

Do you ever hear Daddy say the words "capital gains"?
a) Never
b) Sometimes
c) Only when he's cursing about taxes
d) That is the name of our yacht

What is the most popular subject at your school?
a) Survival
b) Lawn maintenance
c) Photography
d) Tax law

What is your favorite playground activity?
a) Kicking dirt
b) Swinging
c) Feeding the pony
d) Handicapping the pony market

At which weapon are you most skilled?
a) Uzi
b) Glock
c) Archery
d) Litigation

Where do you go on vacation?
a) Detroit
b) Delaware
c) Disney World
d) *Actual* Disney World, the secret recreation planet

How do you spend your summers?
a) Foraging
b) Helping family members cross
c) Hunting big game
d) Hunting foraging children and their family members

What do you want to be when you grow up?
a) Alive
b) A cowboy
c) A doctor
d) Immortal

Calculate your score:
a = 0   b = 1   c = 2   d = 10

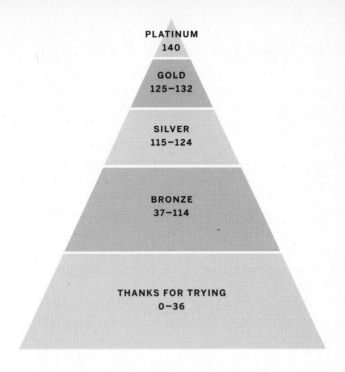

PLATINUM: Why are you wasting your time taking a test?

GOLD: Your family has plenty of this stashed away and plating your fixtures.

SILVER: There is hope. Try lying on a few applications or blackmailing an authority figure.

BRONZE: Your options are professional athlete or military service.

THANKS FOR TRYING: The authorities are on their way.

3.7 **Obesity: Big Thoughts on Big People**

....

WE WOULD like to give our readers a brief history of hunger. It seems everyone in the world has been well fed since the dawn of humanity, and then suddenly, in 1984, Bob Geldof discovered hunger in Ethiopia. He gathered some friends together and recorded a song called "Do They Know It's Christmas?" and played it for the hungry people, because apparently music cures hunger. When hunger returned a year later, they realized they forgot to serve dessert, so some Americans threw together "We Are the World," and hunger was wiped from the face of the earth.

But now hunger is back, and this time it's serious, because it has moved beyond third-world nations and begun affecting first-world people—you know, people that *matter.* Headlines across the West increasingly warn of worldwide food shortages, with sharp jumps in the price of rice and wheat. A major U.S. grocery chain recently limited shoppers to buying 80 pounds* of rice per visit. We don't know about you, but the thought of North Americans being limited to 80 pounds of starch with their evening meal sends shivers up our spines, and we don't want to wait until each of us is restricted to twenty large pizzas per lunch break before we do something about it.

Of course the logical solution would be to eat less, but . . . well, seriously, like that's going to happen on its own. In 2008, for the first time in history, the obese people on the planet began to outnumber the starving people. One would think that North Americans and Africans could find

---

* 36.3 kilograms. Get used to it.

common ground in their constant obsession with finding food, but until someone proposes a plan for the obese people to simply eat the starving people, it seems each continent will have to fend for itself.

According to the Canada Party Institute of Shit We Make Up, North Americans rank their needs in the following order:

1   Television
2   Thousands and thousands of calories daily
3   Porn
    [. . .]
132   Absorbent pads
133   Dinosaur movies
134   Garnish vegetables

For our part, we intend to repurpose America's second-largest civilian employer to address the serious health issues of poor eating habits and a sedentary lifestyle. That's right—the U.S. Postal Service will finally be delivering good news.

CANAFACT

The Canadian national dish, poutine, is comprised of french/freedom fries, gravy, and cheese curds. The International Olympic Committee has classified Canadian cuisine as an extreme sport.

As grocery stores have embraced the vitamin-free world of food substitutes, consumers can no longer discern between a fish, a fish stick, and a stick. But with its sophisticated distribution network and relative efficiency (compared to Congress and Parliament), the U.S. Mail is ideally suited to distribute healthy, local food to nearly every American on a daily basis, meaning the Postal Service—now the Food Service—will at last transport something worth the postage.

This new operation will also provide a valuable service to our farmers and alternative-energy industries. When citizens claim their daily food package, they will return vegetable refuse from previous deliveries, which will be converted to biofuel and compost at the repurposed postal facilities. These facilities will fuel the entire vehicle fleet and generate vast quantities of fresh, nutrient-rich soil to replace the chemicals and synthetic fertilizers that are destroying our farmland and waterways. (Our apologies to Monsanto, who for more than a century have [TEXT REDACTED].)*

IT'S A PROMISE!

☞ Fast-food mascots must be thematically tied to the nutritional value of the product they're selling. Everyone, please give a warm welcome to Ronald McInsulin.

But what good is nutritious food without daily exercise? It's no secret that we've become a continent of torpid slackers (what some might call a "broken escalator," others might call "stairs"). Enter stage two of our plan to make the postal service a lid for America's cookie jar. Rather than drop daily meals on your doorstep, our drivers will cruise "ice-cream-truck-style" down the street, enticing consumers to chase their supper by playing "Peanut Butter Jelly Time" over the loudspeaker. Not only will this aid a proportional exercise-to-caloric-intake ratio, but an endless (and endlessly hilarious) string of iPhone videos capturing fat people doing "dinner sprints" will launch a whole new class of YouTube channels.

---

* Not even kidding here, we are scared to death to make a joke about Monsanto.

3.8 **All We Are Saying Is Give Guns a Chance**

DESPITE CANADA'S pathetic attempt to arm its civilians—a paltry two hundred or so gun deaths in Canada each year, compared to America's impressive ten thousand plus—we recognize that the United States is steeped in gun culture, and we wouldn't dream of infringing on Americans' second-amendment right to live in fear of British troops rolling up on their shore with a discounted shipment of Royal Family commemorative plates.

We will, in fact, support the notion of "gun rights" to a greater extent than any administration since Teddy Roosevelt's "Hatriot Act" of 1902. And by that, we mean guns will now have rights of their own. For decades, guns have been slandered by left-wing bullet-dodgers as somehow being responsible for killing people when they are really just doing what they were designed to do: kill people.

CANAFACT
Out of politeness, all Canadian guns have built-in silencers.

As guns actually outnumber Americans now, we believe firearms are long overdue for protection from the people who use them. We are pleased to announce our Bill of Rights for Guns, affectionately known around the office as "Every Gun a Loaded Gun."

I   Guns shall not be used as a substitute for a penis, no matter how small, sad, and lonely said penis may be.

II   Guns are not people, but they share the basic human right to be loud and careless when mixed with alcohol.

III   Guns shall not be made to kill things that are smaller than they are. Asking your AK-47 to shoot a rabbit belittles your weapon and poisons the stew.

IV   Guns have the right to misfire if they choose, particularly in cases where they have been loaded with the wrong ammunition or against their will.

V   Same-caliber guns have an inalienable right to share a drawer, just like socks, earrings, and two-piece swimsuits.

VI   Teenagers shall be educated in proper gun use, including holstering, trigger locks, and abstaining from guns altogether.

VII   Guns shall not be sent to fight in wars on falsified intelligence to serve a political agenda, and should they make the ultimate sacrifice, government shall make no rule preventing their broken barrels from being shown on the evening news.

IT'S A PROMISE!

☞ The Second Amendment doesn't say anything about ammunition. Introducing our BLAMMO policy—Balanced Limits on Ammo.

||||||||||||||||||||||||||||||||||||||||||||||||||||||

VIII Every gun is entitled to shelter and basic preventive care— nothing fancy, just a box and some regular lube—so that we may keep guns off the streets.

IX   Guns have the right to be gathered in groups, organized for piece-ful assembly, and, providing they pose no physical threat, to shoot their mouths off without fear of being muzzled.

X   It should go without saying, but guns have the right to keep and bear other guns. (Within reason.)

3.9 Crime and Punishment, and then Crime Again

AMERICA HAS done a terrific job keeping criminals off the streets by making prison such a fashionable option. Accounting for only 5 percent of the world's population, the U.S. can boast 23 percent of the world's prisoners (the most on earth), with more than 3 percent of U.S. adults incarcerated, on probation, or on parole. As we have no first-hand experience with the American prison system, we must conclude from these statistics that being incarcerated is incredibly fun, and U.S. citizens don't really "go to jail," they are just taking a "vacation from crime."

Still, it seems a bit spendy to drop more than $60 billion a year managing these tranquil retreats, much of it going to private corrections companies that have created business models that finally make crime pay. Fortunately, these companies' profits are cycled back into the economy through millions in political donations and lobbying the government for longer prison sentences so these trendy corrections-cabanas won't go to waste.

We also find it unsporting that so many attendees don't really *earn* their vacation, taking advantage of the "War on Drugs" to sneak into prison without really doing anything wrong. And while we understand that the black man in America has had a rough time, it's unfair to the other races that they are hogging jail cells at six times the rate of deserving white folk.

🍁 **CANAFACT**

Many Canadian criminals are sentenced to Brett Ratner movie marathons. The recidivism rate in Canada is the lowest in the world.

We realize how unpopular it would be to close these barbed-wire Disneylands and prevent future freeloaders through radical and inexpensive ideas like sports and music programs for children. However, since more than half of these inmates take this holiday more than once, and many of them vacation for years—even decades—at a time, it seems far too easy to take advantage of the current system.

Which is why we've developed a four-step Canada Party "Working Vacations" plan to close the loopholes that currently allow 2.3 million citizens to lounge on the tax-payers' dime:

Step one: Legalize "the Kind," tax the shit out of it, and use the proceeds to elevate impoverished children instead of waiting around to debase them as adults. (See Chapter 4.5, "Weed. Sweet, Sweet Weed.")

Step two: Make criminals earn their way into prison the same way karaoke singers earn their fifteen minutes of fame and thirty years of drug abuse: through nationally televised talent shows. By combining our love of contest shows with the thirst for justice, criminals can participate in *American Idol*-style trials broadcast in an episodic for-mat. Citizens will judge by text message, with the sentence carried out on next week's program.* The texting fees brought in by each criminal will pay for their entire prison vacay. This is true participatory justice.

Step three: Rather than relaxing in the sunny prison yard and savoring daily body-cavity searches (it's like a cin-derblock Fire Island!), prisoners will enjoy their working

---

* Finalists will perform a duet with Dog the Bounty Hunter.

vacation by producing food and power for their local community. Prison land will be converted to greenhouses and orchards, and inmates taught every aspect of farming. Weight rooms will be wired to convert all that wasted human energy into electricity. The Bureau of Prisons will contract with alternative-energy companies to train inmates as technicians for solar and wind technology. The inmates will be paid minimum wage for building these devices—greatly reducing the cost of producing alternative energy—with 90 percent of their income held in escrow until their release.

Step four: Citizens will emerge from their working vacation fit, well nourished, highly skilled, and with savings in the bank. Parole officers will coordinate with farms and the same alternative-energy companies to hire these trained, experienced growers and technicians to go straight to work for a decent, living wage. As these workers achieve seniority, they will return to prisons to train and mentor future farmers and technicians.

IT'S A PROMISE!

☞ We will allow one abortion for every person on death row. Congratulations, Texas—you are now home to Six Flags Over Planned Parenthood.

We realize, of course, that this system doesn't work for everybody. There will always be a small percentage of inmates who aren't so into planting trees as they are into raping and murdering them. For these special clients, we are working on a "Fighting Vacations" plan to augment our brave soldiers serving in conflicts around the world. If America's enemies don't like facing our best citizens, let's see how they like it when we send them our worst.

TREATING EXPERTS LIKE MAMMALS

AN IDEOLOGICAL THROWDOWN!

4.1 Grandpa Lost His Shins in the Big One: Our Statute of Limitations on Living Off Other People's Sacrifices

SOONER OR later we need to accept that the "Greatest Generation" was about two generations ago, and we have since been riding the coattails of our grandparents' valor. At some point in the past fifty years, we decided our species had sacrificed enough and it was time to enjoy ourselves at the expense of our own grandchildren, like the guy who brings nothing to the party, hits on the host's girlfriend, then pukes on her dress on the way out. And that's what we're saying to our grandkids: "Thanks for the fun, sorry about the mess—but for what it's worth, the endangered sea bass was delicious."

We honor the sacrifices of our forebears with speeches and monuments, but not with our actions. And since we've inherited our luxuries instead of earning them, we are only a sweaty glacier away from being deprived of the things we think we can't live without, like Starbucks and flat-screens and all the children we can spawn. We *need* things like water, food, clothing, and shelter; we only *want* them to be bottled water, shark-fin soup, designer labels, and houses that would make cavemen wonder where their children went wrong.

It's impractical to suggest that we can return to a culture of deprivation when our kids think the right to keep and bear PlayStations is in the Constitution. But to stop the spiraling cycle of waste and debt, Canada would like to help America (and itself) find creative ways to turn our unearned luxuries into community reinvestments with the handy *Canada Party Guide to Turning Our Unearned Luxuries into Community Reinvestments.**

Sample programs include:

Meals on Hot Wheels: We applaud the good folks at NAS-CAR for their recent environmental efforts, such as experimenting with ethanol, fuel injection, and unleaded gasoline. Still, it's hard to defend as "sustainable" a vehicle that gets less than five miles per gallon when it's doing what it was designed to do.

We will return NASCAR to its roots as a means of evading the police when delivering bootleg alcohol from town to town. Instead of alcohol, however, they will deliver meals to shut-ins, combining the thrills of two-hundred-

---

* The woman who names our manuals is on vacation.

mile-per-hour racing with the societal benefit of feeding the elderly at Santa-like speeds. We predict this will also be a boon to NASCAR's fan base, who have grown tired of watching cars speed around in endless circles, leading to a common medical condition in the South known as "Chevy Eyes."

Real World: Outer Space: There is no arguing the technological and self-esteem benefits of our space programs, and NASA has proved particularly efficient at setting golf-distance records in low-gravity environments. But NASA costs taxpayers about $18 billion a year, without the benefit of Tiger-sized endorsement deals. (When is Nike going to wake up to the potential for "Aerospace Jordans"?)

We will require NASA to include one ordinary person on every space mission—and by "ordinary," we mean "character," and by "character," we mean "stereotype caricature"—a loud, middle-aged black woman, or a hair-gel-addicted perennial spring-breaker who constantly asks the astronauts, "Where all the green women at?" The footage from these missions will be edited into half-hour narratives for the reality-television market, providing an untapped revenue stream for NASA and a new direction for the space-drama genre, replacing CGI with slow-witted, camera-friendly douchebags.

> **IT'S A PROMISE!**
>
> ☞ Citizens must earn the right to vote by giving one year of national service. Inner-city schoolteachers will be given their vote automatically, plus a cake and a heartfelt apology.

Casino Royalzheimer's: America's aging population presents a unique challenge to the U.S. economy. Social Security and Medicare/Medicaid are two of the largest government programs on the planet, accounting for 40 percent of the federal budget. But where bean-counters see an obstacle, we see an opportunity to corral—and profit from—our senior citizens.

Our plan will create a network of government-owned casinos in Arizona and Florida devoted exclusively to retirees, where our elders can gamble away their social security entitlements before Bible salesmen and greedy children can get to them. The soft-earned retirement benefits that these seniors lose at the craps table will go right back into the system, ensuring there will be sufficient government funds for next month's paycheck, and the cycle begins again. The casinos will provide all the necessities for a cushy retiree lifestyle: free buffets, shuttle service to prevent seniors from driving, and a weekly production of *Matlock on Ice*—just long enough of a break that old people will forget they had already seen it.

4.2 What to Do with "the Gays"

OVER THE YEARS, countless polls and surveys have attempted to gauge how Americans feel about Canada. The answers vary with the tone of the question—for instance, Americans have a low opinion of Canada's universal health care when they hear about waiting lists for bionic hair and solid-gold hip replacements, but are generally impressed that, unlike in the United States, no one in Canada dies from a sore throat.

For decades, however, one answer has repeated itself on poll after poll, survey after survey, late-night talk show after late-night talk show. When asked, point blank, their "general impression" of Canada, Americans have consistently responded with a single phrase: "Pretty gay."

Canadians consider themselves quite tough, and usually react to this comment with what passes for outrage in Canada (a heavy sigh and changing the channel). But in 2005, the nation took the "If you can't beat 'em..." approach, and became the fourth country in the world to legalize same-sex marriage.

Nearly half of Americans feel that marriage must comprise solely a man and a woman, no matter how gay one or both of them actually are. Although that number shrinks every year as citizens become—what's the right word here—"informed," we do realize that centuries of religious intolerance cannot be swept away overnight by something as unfamiliar as—what's the right word here—"information."

> **IT'S A PROMISE!**
>
> ☞ One gay couple will be allowed to marry for each straight couple that gets divorced. Congratulations, Las Vegas—you are now the gayest city in America.

The cornerstone of the argument against allowing homosexuals to marry is that sexual promiscuity among gays will destroy traditional marriage. Somehow, through a mathematical formula we have yet to grasp, this means the best way to stop gays from having multiple sexual partners is to deny them the one institution that would prevent them from having multiple sexual partners.*

We accept that there are plenty of things about America that Canadians will simply never be able to grasp, so in

---

* This is the same logic behind the idea that contraception somehow causes abortions, but we digress.

an attempt to be fair to the type of people who think *you* shouldn't be allowed to eat cake because *they* are on a diet, we offer the following compromise on gay marriage:

For every straight couple that divorces, one gay couple will be allowed to marry. This system reverses the correlation between gay marriage and traditional marriage, allowing gays to marry only when traditional marriage has failed first. Rather than gay couples destroying traditional marriage, the failure of a traditional marriage will create a legally wed gay couple.

🍁 CANAFACT

Canada legalized gay marriage to preserve body heat during ice-fishing excursions. Canadian men love dipping their poles in ice holes.

We understand that there will be resistance to this idea, and if the plan proves too unpopular, we will simply institute our *Children of Men* policy: since all gay babies come from straight couples, we will declare all straight marriages illegal. Only gays will be allowed to marry, as they are the only couples that have the proven ability to not conceive gay babies. Within a generation, the entire argument will be rendered moot. Now *that's* progress!

A secondary concern about legalizing gay marriage is that it will lead to cross-species mating, an idea famously endorsed by U.S. senator Rick "I've Had Sex Eight Times in My Life" Santorum. Although Canada has enjoyed gay marriage for less than a decade, and cross-species mating is generally restricted to our colder provinces, to date we've seen no correlation between the two.

However, should America indeed skip down that road of bestiality, holding hands with possums, butterflies, and other members of the sluttier species, we believe this would be a good thing for gay marriage. Once people become accustomed to women enjoying romantic picnics with bears and men tapping maple trees for a taste of love syrup, then human-human unions—regardless of gender—will seem almost quaint.

In the event that this unlikely scenario becomes likely, all interested parties can refer to *The Canada Party Guide to Marital Rights for Cross-Species Couples* for guidance. For example, if you are exploring a potential non-*sapiens* relationship, you might want to familiarize yourself with certain passages from our "Qualifying Species" chapter:

SECTION 1.8.2: Special tax incentives will permit cross-species relationships involving animals and plants that invite a sense of patriotism. Mating is encouraged for: North America beavers (*Castor canadensis*), moose (inclusive), bald eagles (*Haliaeetus leucocephalus*), bears (excluding pandas, due to immigration issues), maple trees, and captive sea creatures demonstrating advanced playful-splashing abilities. Please note: the nonhuman party must pay annual property taxes on all nests, dens, forest glens, migratory residences (if occupied for more than three consecutive months), parks, and frequented bodies of water. Please direct inquiries to the Internal Revenue Service, Division of Natural Domiciles.

4.3 You Are NOT the Father! Abstinence-Only Education and the Rise of Immaculate Conceptions

THE RISE in teen pregnancies in states that forbid schools to teach contraception has us completely baffled. Despite the prevalence of abstinence-only education programs, teenagers are still getting pregnant, even though they are not having sex. In response to this growing trend, we are pleased to announce our own program, "Abstinence Plus!"—a comprehensive strategy to battle all proven and suspected causes of pregnancy. Please note the following improvements we're bringing to abstinence protocol:

IT'S A PROMISE!

☞ Sex education in schools must acknowledge that there is such a thing as sex.

1　Prohibitions against sexual contact between teenagers will be extended to other risky behavior, such as tandem bicycles, piggyback rides, and doubles tennis. Should a situation arise in which teenagers need to hold hands—a rescue attempt from a burning building, for example—they should be wearing gloves that have been blessed by the local parson and retain physical contact only as long as it takes to hum the national anthem.

2　To appeal to modern youth, the "Purity Ring" campaign will be renamed "Purity Bling," and expanded to include purity haircuts, purity piercings, purity sock puppets, and purity sandwich boards. Additionally, our friends at Adidas have agreed to launch a line of purity high-tops in time for the Christmas shopping season.

3　The rash of teen pregnancies following Janet Jackson's wardrobe malfunction at the 2004 Super Bowl (a.k.a. "Nipplegeddon") proved the deleterious effects of sexualized programming on adolescents. Last year, a fifteen-year-old Chicago youth spontaneously gave birth to twins after watching a *Gossip Girl* marathon. Henceforth, we recommend teenagers use the calendar method to inform their viewing habits.

4 We encourage parents of teenage girls to download our forthcoming iPhone application, "iBod," to their teenager's cell phone. The iBod monitors your daughter's cycle, emitting a tachyon pulse at the moment of ovulation, bending the space-time continuum to lock her into a state of permanent menses. A version for teenage boys—the iMpotent—is still in the testing stage.

5 Despite our respect for abstinence-only education, we have decided to look into the advantages of condom use as well, and recommend that boys of reproductive age wear condoms at all times while they are being abstinent.

4.4 Media Libs

AS WESTERN MEDIA organizations demand an increasing margin of forgiveness to accompany their decreasing standards of journalism, news cycles have fallen into a predictable pattern of call-and-response report-

IT'S A PROMISE!

☞ Pundits may not call themselves journalists, any more than evangelists can call themselves gods.

age. While the newsrooms have become more polarized, the stories themselves have become more similar. To make journalists' jobs even easier, we are creating a series of "Media Libs," which are Mad Libs for journalists to use when they are late for a deadline. Or busy. Or just don't give a shit anymore. An example:

The End of (noun) Control.

The (noun) control controversy is far from over. The government-mandated withdrawal of (adj.) (noun) took effect today, leaving millions of Americans (verb) in disbelief that this day has truly come. At precisely nine o'clock this morning, state officials (verb) retailers to (verb) any and all remaining (adj.) (noun) and (noun) from their shelves. The targeted retailers were those who had publicly vowed to keep providing these (adj.) products to their clients.

For days leading up to the raid, (noun) began (verb) what they could, worried that this option could be (verb) forever. With penalties in place for purchasing (noun), many users decided to go north, to Canada, where the long winters make such (noun) necessary and abundant. The Canadians, known for (adj.) (verb) American policy, have announced the discontinuance does not apply to them. This is expected to cause American (noun) to (verb) their way to Canada to (verb) their (noun) legally. Canadian men are opening their arms and zippers at the thought of countless (adj.)-age American (noun) flooding across the border for (adj.) stays.

Opposition to the legislation was fierce, and groups across North America (verb) to protect the (noun) of users. In Michigan alone, thirteen people were (verb) for (verb)-ing. There are exceptions, as a (noun) can qualify for a legal (noun) if they agree to be subject to a (adj.) ultrasound. Proponents of the law want to take it a step further by requiring a/an (noun) to replace the suffering (noun) would otherwise experience with a dozen (noun).

NOUNS	ADJECTIVES	VERBS	ADVERBS
man/men	state	protest	unfairly
woman/women	local	arrest	ignorantly
fetus	federal	beaten	secretly
Congressman	elitist	warn	sanctimoniously
drug war	Islamist	stockpile	constitutionally
contraceptive	free-market	loiter	candidly
socialist	dangerous	condemn	religiously
terrorist	black	dissent	economically
activist judge	Latino	discriminate	illegally
gun locker	free	deport	covertly
altar boy	indeterminate	shock	racially
Nazi	transvaginal	torture	politically
vagina	transanal	waterboard	electorally
hip-hop	transrectal	Cheney	severely
school lunch	transurethral	pray	embarrassingly
rights	transnasal	evolve	audaciously
Adam and Steve	rogue	strip-search	fast
freedom	undocumented	body-scan	hard
liberty	constitutional	rapture	exhaustingly
ammunition	genetically modified	canonize	punctually
episiotomy		occupy	optimistically
prison term	same-sex	occupado	strategically
patriot	un-American	pander	feasibly
Founding Father	liberal	vote	comically
hoodie	conservative	elect	painfully
Oklahoma	libertarian	impeach	armageddony
	minty		

4.5 Weed. Sweet, Sweet Weed.

SERIOUSLY, AMERICA. Seriously.

We will legalize it, tax it, use the profits to buy stock in Cheetos, and then use that money to buy America back from China. We will declare a purchasing minimum age of thirty-five years (with the same laws against selling to minors that work so well for alcohol and cigarettes), so the only things pot will be a gateway to is middle age and relief from back pain.

IT'S A PROMISE!

☞ Like drugs and cigarettes, each new piece of legislation must clearly state its possible side effects.

Gangs and drug cartels in the U.S. and throughout the Americas will lose a primary source of funding. Crime rates and inner-city violence will fall dramatically. Billions of dollars wasted on the War on Drugs will be redirected to prevention and rehabilitation programs. The thousands of inmates serving time for minor possession charges will be given their lives back.

Are we high as we write this? Yes, we are. Are we robbing convenience stores, eating babies, and running Ponzi schemes to bilk homeowners out of their mortgages? No, we're not. We're relaxing, being creative, and savoring this pizza, which—for some reason—tastes like it was hand-tossed by the Dalai Lama and baked in a solar flare.

Sorry, what were we talking about again?

4.6 The Constitution, Annotated

IT IS COMMON knowledge that the U.S. Constitution established a functioning federal government in 1787 and was then amended with the Bill of Rights in 1789 to protect citizens from the systemic abuses that only a fully functioning government can wreak.

Canada—though still somewhat Britishy at the time—was enjoying a brief period of semi-neutrality between the 1783 Treaty of Paris and the War of 1812. James Madison, fearing the anti-federalists would find a way to dissolve the newly united American colonies, decided to send an original copy of the Bill of Rights for safekeeping to the governor general of Canada, a man who had gotten him hooked on the original frontier edition of Angry Birds.

🍁 **CANAFACT**

Angry Birds is based on the Revolutionary War tactic of catapulting messenger pigeons across enemy lines to prevent them from being brought down by British snipers.

Unbeknownst to most Americans, these original documents included a corresponding Bill of Responsibilities to accompany the Bill of Rights, because according to the cover letter written by Madison, "OMG I can totes see this country becoming a whiny bunch of teat-suckers." A janitor working in the Canadian Parliament building recently found these papers while sneaking a lunch doobie in an abandoned storage room.

Fortuitously timed for our new reign over America, we propose—in keeping with the original intent of the Founding Fathers—to restore the details of these responsibilities to each amendment:

AMENDMENT I

Congress shall make no law respecting an establishment of religion, or prohibiting the free exercise thereof; or abridging the freedom of speech, or of the press; or the right of the people peaceably to assemble, and to petition the government for a redress of grievances.

The people shall make no shield of religion, or prohibit common sense from trumping the right to fondle altar boys; or claim free speech includes the right to lie; or conduct peacefully assembled flash mobs that block traffic when we are running late.

AMENDMENT II

A well regulated militia, being necessary to the security of a free state, the right of the people to keep and bear arms, shall not be infringed.

The people shall not ignore the "well regulated" part of this amendment when asserting their constitutional right to brandish automatic weapons when picking their children up from preschool.

AMENDMENT III

No soldier shall, in time of peace be quartered in any house, without the consent of the owner, nor in time of war, but in a manner to be prescribed by law.

No citizen shall, in time of peace, war, or metaphorical war, pretend that preaching racism and xenophobia qualifies as "supporting the troops."

AMENDMENT IV

The right of the people to be secure in their persons, houses, papers, and effects, against unreasonable searches and seizures, shall not be violated, and no Warrants shall issue, but upon probable cause, supported by Oath or affirmation, and particularly describing the place to be searched, and the persons or things to be seized.

Citizens are expected to be smart about hiding their weed.

AMENDMENT V

No person shall be held to answer for a capital, or otherwise infamous crime, unless on a presentment or indict-
ment of a Grand Jury, except in cases arising in the land
or naval forces, or in the Militia, when
in actual service in time of War or public danger; nor shall any person be subject for the same offense to be twice put
in jeopardy of life or limb; nor shall be
compelled in any criminal case to be a
witness against himself, nor be deprived
of life, liberty, or property, without due
process of law; nor shall private prop-
erty be taken for public use, without just compensation.

> **IT'S A PROMISE!**
>
> ☞ **All new legislation must be titled to reflect its actual contents. The Patriot Act will be renamed "Fuck You, Thomas Jefferson."**

The public shall not pervert these rights by attribut-
ing criminal activity to noncriminal acts, such as wear-
ing a hoodie, riding a skateboard, gathering in groups, or
walking through Arizona.

AMENDMENT VI

In all criminal prosecutions, the accused shall enjoy the
right to a speedy and public trial, by an impartial jury of
the State and district wherein the crime shall have been
committed, which district shall have been previously
ascertained by law, and to be informed of the nature and
cause of the accusation; to be confronted with the witnesses against him; to have compulsory process for obtain-
ing witnesses in his favor, and to have the Assistance of
Counsel for his defence.

Wealthy citizens shall not use their money and con-
nections to draw out legal processes to such an absurd

level that it breaks the system, leaving poor citizens with the choice of being white or going to prison.

AMENDMENT VII

In Suits at common law, where the value in controversy shall exceed twenty dollars, the right of trial by jury shall be preserved, and no fact tried by a jury, shall be otherwise re-examined in any Court of the United States, than according to the rules of the common law.

The public, particularly the media, shall not convict fellow citizens in the court of public opinion based on something they saw on Geraldo.

AMENDMENT VIII

Excessive bail shall not be required, nor excessive fines imposed, nor cruel and unusual punishments inflicted.

Citizens shall not do things that make us want to be cruel and unusual.

AMENDMENT IX

The enumeration in the Constitution, of certain rights, shall not be construed to deny or disparage others retained by the people.

The public shall acknowledge that "the people" includes immigrants, gays, and women.

AMENDMENT X

The powers not delegated to the United States by the Constitution, nor prohibited by it to the states, are reserved to the states respectively, or to the people.

The states and the people shall be worthy of the rights granted them, and not douche it up for everybody. (We're looking at you, Florida.)

4.7 **Science vs. Religion**
(Spoiler: Science Wins in Overtime!)

....

THE GREAT theologian Bertrand Russell told us there are two kinds of morality: the kind we preach but do not practice, and the kind we practice but do not preach. Unfortunately, it is preaching morality, not practicing it, that gets you elected. This is why candidates preach about getting the government out of your private life, but once elected, practice an inflexible set of rules on how you must treat your vagina and with whom you may share it.

The very concept of "morality" has become a political tool. Worse, morality has been hijacked by religion, so that it is no longer possible to be independently moral on the national stage—a candidate has to issue press releases on little notepads that say "from the desk of God." It's been noted that even President Obama scored votes because of his resemblance to Jesus: a dark-skinned socialist who fights poverty, offers free health care, turns the other cheek, and is crucified by out-of-touch white guys who think the world is flat.

The claim of superior morality is the grand magic trick of the election process, a sleight of hand that elevates a candidate to greatness because he can wiggle his fingers and pull a Holy Spirit out of his hat. Meanwhile, the audience doesn't notice that the food was overpriced, the drinks were watered down, and the performer neglected to supply a feasible plan for withdrawal from the Middle East. Candidates who claim moral superiority over their opponent

> **IT'S A PROMISE!**
>
> ☞ Anyone who questions evolutionary genetics will have to explain the Neanderthal uncle in every family.
>
> ||||||||||||||||||||||||||||||||||||||||||||||

are basically saying, "Sorry about the wars, the debt, and the poverty, but hey, watch me saw a homosexual in half!"

The true Houdinis of politics—and these guys really should be headlining in Vegas—are those who can misdirect the audience to be wary of their own senses by attacking rationality itself. They will tell you that faith is a sensory organ and evidence is just opinion wearing a lab coat. Their followers are easy to spot (global warming deniers, Tim Tebow fans) but impossible to reason with, because they believe in their party politics the way children believe in Santa: "It doesn't matter if your platform contradicts all rational thought, I'll support it as long as there's something under the tree for *me*."

Beware any candidate who tells you that God and science are on the opposite sides of a mud pit in some universal tug of war. Science is the means by which we grow as a civilization, and faith unites us as a community to make that growth mean something. They are no more in conflict than the gravitational forces between the earth and the moon, each steadying the orbit of the other but governed by different atmospheric rules. Which is why attempting to "prove" the existence of God makes faith as useless as a lunar hurricane monitor, while praying for divine intervention in our daily lives reduces God to a concierge with attention deficit disorder.

🍁 **CANAFACT**

Canadians prefer to piss each other off with unintelligible accents rather than bringing God into it.

Our administration will not be a religious institution, but it will be a moral one. We will thus create two distinct bodies to regulate these differences: the Department of Faith and the Department of Reason.

Canada has a proud tradition of religious tolerance. We believe a Jew even lived here once. But religion is also a business, and if the government has to protect consumers from things like raw milk and naughty language on the television, then the Department of Faith will protect them from things they actually need protection from.

For instance, if you want to put $50 million a year into your church's "Funny Hat Division," that's fine, but you have to be transparent to the investors who pay your bills and eat your crackers. You will purchase www.funnyhat-division.com, you will detail your expenditures on the site, you will show it to that sweet old lady who gives you half her pension every month, and you will let her decide whether those hats are really worth the comedy.

The Department of Reason will oversee all of the government's programs that rely on faith-free rational thought, protecting citizens from faith-based influence in what should be purely rational matters. Sex education for teens will cease to resemble a kindergarten magic show. Gays will be considered human rather than "almost." Climate change will no longer be dismissed as God's plan for polar bears. Pedophiles will be prosecuted no matter how funny their hat is.

Should an issue come about that cannot be handled by one of these departments, the opposing parties will settle the matter through a "friendly" game of hockey (see Chapter 1.5, "Understanding Hockey, from the Country That Gave You Football and Basketball").

4.8 Living in Fear: The War of the Words

BELOW IS a brief (and incomplete) list of entities with whom, according to Fox News, America is at war:

Terror	Kids
Marriage	Ladies' night
Christmas	Conservative women
Hanukkah	Fishermen
Easter	Salt
Halloween	Spuds
Fall holidays	Sugary drinks
Fossil fuels	Chocolate milk
The Constitution	Food*

As we† systematically replace our journalists with pundits, we shouldn't be surprised that news metaphors increasingly lean toward the hyperbolic. It's hard to find a story about "sharing" anymore that does not invoke the specter of communism, and the next kitten caught in a tree will probably be reported as "the War on Mittens."

The *real* metaphorical war—the war to trend all wars—is the war on language, an ideological blitzkrieg to colonize our vocabulary by elevating every minor difference of opinion into a battle for your children's souls. Every offense is a hate crime, every tragedy a holocaust, every

---

* There are apparently two-front wars on the food items in this list.

† The North American "we."

protest a revolution, every critic a Nazi. It's no wonder we are all scared shitless; the only good news we hear anymore is that Armageddon has been delayed because Satan and Exxon had a scheduling conflict.

It's not a stretch to picture this as a long-term effect of the nineties political correctness craze, which gave us firepersons, Ebonics, and the hyphenated American. But we let a good thing get the best of us, and before long the obligation to respect people's differences mutated into a requirement to respect their opinions, then their exaggerations, and then their lies. Over time, media organizations (formerly known as "the News") discovered there was ratings gold in giving airtime to the chronically obtuse, and Rush Limbaugh never had to worry about money again.

So we turned to our comedy shows, of all places, to find sources we can trust, because our news anchors stopped taming lions and started cramming increasingly obese clowns into increasingly tiny cars. As our discourse became absurd beyond rational debate, we took up satire as the only available rhetorical strategy. Imagine if our grandparents had considered *Laugh-In* a reliable source of information because they just couldn't trust that Cronkite fellow. Imagine if our parents believed *60 Minutes* was biased toward hour-lovers, and tuned in to *Saturday Night Live*'s "Weekend Update" to confirm that Generalissimo Francisco Franco was still dead.

Over the past decade, we have ceased operating within a common frame of irony, no longer able tell the logical from the ridiculous. How much more evidence do we need than the fact that, at some point in the 2012 Republican primaries, Newt "Third Time's a Charm" Gingrich became the spokesman for the sanctity of marriage? Somewhere in heaven—whether because he lost all faith in humanity, or because punch lines were never so obvious when he was alive—George Carlin wept.

The American Dream—once a simple romantic comedy—has been released on DVD as a horror film, with director's commentary by the Mayans that roughly translates as "You're all pretty fucked." Our paranoia extends far beyond fringe terrors like the idea that Dick Clark's death means there will be no more new years. We've built an artificial network of panic-perches from which we squawk about the evils of evolutionism, health care, education, sustainability, basic human kindness, and—somehow—Muppets and Dr. Seuss.

Even in Canada the war of the words has been elevated to a dizzying state, with foreign speculators branding the unconscionably dirty tar sands as "Ethical Oil" and portraying local environmentalists as part of some radical terrorist network. It wasn't long ago that Canada was like Mayberry, where the constable wouldn't let you out of a parking ticket until you tried a slice of Aunt Bee's pie. But Andy and Opie have gone fishing with the boys, and here as in America, the Barney Fifes are taking over.

IT'S A PROMISE!

☞ We will implement a new "Talk to Strangers" policy. Neighborhoods with the most shared lawnmowers will receive a complimentary pancake breakfast, served by your elected officials.

It is time to act, and we are asking Americans to help us fight the good fight. Reclaim your natural right to rational discourse and sensible governance. Reclaim your constitutional title of "We the people," and remind your government and media that they answer to *you*. Reclaim your great nation. And then put us in charge of it.

Thanks for reading, and keep an eye out for our next book: *I Am the Lorax, I Speak for the Terrorists.*

APPENDICES

APPENDIX A
SOME HANDY TEAR-OUT
APPLICATION FORMS

WE CAN'T fix everything on the first day. So until we get around to the little things, we will be streamlining the hiring of civil service employees with tear-out applications in keeping with current hiring standards. Samples below:

Application for Supreme Court Justice

....

CONGRATULATIONS ON your nomination to the United States Supreme Court! To streamline the process and avoid contentious confirmation hearings, please fill out the following application.

With which law school are you affiliated?
a) Yale
b) Harvard
c) Columbia
d) I withdraw my application

In what way would you bring diversity to the Supreme Court?
a) I am a woman
b) I am a visible minority
c) Both a) and b)
d) I tan well

What aesthetic deficiencies might make you a target of partisan attacks?
a) Weight problem
b) Height problem
c) Excessive mustache (women)
d) Insufficient mustache (men)

What might reflect poorly on your character during the nomination process?
a) Former oil company lobbyist
b) Secret affair with intern
c) Secret affair with oil company lobbyist
d) I own all of Nickelback's albums

What do you like best about the Constitution?
a) The gun parts
b) The gay parts
c) It's all good
d) Fixing it

If you could add one item to the Constitution, what would it be?
a) The right to keep and bear more things
b) Quiz restrictions on Facebook
c) A more marketable title
d) An index

Would you be willing to participate in the Court's "Wacky Robe Friday"?
a) Yes
b) No

What are your views on the death penalty?
a) I support the death penalty
b) I do not support the death penalty
c) I enjoyed *Death to Smoochy*
d) I am against death in all its forms

Do you favor gun control?
a) Yes
b) No
c) It is wrong to infringe on a gun's constitutional rights
d) All guns should wear a leash

What best describes your views on same-sex couples?
a) It is a matter for the states
b) It is a matter for the feds
c) Gays have the right to be as miserable as the rest of us
d) I would enjoy viewing them

What are your views on the separation of church and state?
a) We are a Christian nation
b) We are a secular nation
c) We should skirt the issue by referring to Christian ideology as "the moral center"
d) They are a constant disruption and should not be allowed to sit next to each other

Please choose the abortion stance that describes you best:
a) Pro-choice
b) Anti-abortion
c) Only in cases in which the mother's life is threatened
d) Only in cases in which my nomination is threatened

Do you have Oprah's support?
a) Yes
b) I withdraw my application

Application to Be an Airport Screener for the Transportation Security Administration (TSA)

....

THE WORD "hero" is overused these days, so why not? Let's overuse it some more. Our airport screeners represent the last line of defense between the American people and their irrational fears, protecting travelers from the concepts of dignity and efficiency, which serve as gateway ideals to terrorism. To join our elite band of wand warriors, please submit this document—along with a DNA sample in a single, quart-sized, zip-top, clear plastic bag—to your nearest Homeland Security office.

Why do you want to be an airport screener?
a) I have a healthy respect for luggage
b) So I can force celebrities to talk to me
c) The Gap doesn't have a dental plan
d) That's a suspicious question

What might make you assume someone is a terrorist?
a) Shoddy beard maintenance
b) They have a hat I would never wear

c) My gut says so

d) They speak in unintelligible baby coos

What travel item can most easily be used as a weapon?

a) Tap water

b) A half-full tube of toothpaste

c) Anything that is round or not round

d) Freely expressed political ideology

What previous jobs have prepared you to be an airport screener?

a) Inconvenience Store Clerk

b) Dental Insistent

c) Bee Whisperer

d) Mormon Couples Therapist

What would you like your screener nickname to be?

a) "X-Ray Ray"

b) "Jack the Zipper"

c) "Fondles"

d) "Miss Interpret"

What did you think of the movie *Police Academy*?

a) Changed my life

b) Memorized every line

c) Made me the person I am today

d) Best documentary ever

What would make you add someone's name to the "No Fly" list?

a) I can't pronounce it

b) Gratuitous use of the letter *z*

c) Just feel like being a dick today

d) They didn't bring me anything nice back from their trip

Where do you see yourself in ten years?
a) I don't plan on living that long
b) Producing a reality show about things we find in people's luggage
c) At home admiring my *Guinness*-record-winning collection of confiscated toenail clippers
d) Right here. Doing this.

Application for Congressional Strategist
....

REGARDLESS OF the reigning political party, members of Congress will always need strategists to sell their ideas to the American people. By "sell," we mean "throat-cram," and by "the American people," we mean "gullible yokels who vote according to cat-based internet memes." We are not currently hiring for this position, so in addition to the following application, please submit a cover letter convincing us that we are.

What made you become a political strategist?
a) Karl Rove bought my soul on eBay
b) My degree in Art History is useless
c) I don't trust people with integrity
d) Emperor Palpatine offered me a plate of "Force brownies"

What do you love most about your work?
a) Covering up sex scandals
b) Creating sex scandals
c) The lying
d) Getting caught lying and then lying my way out of it

How would you overcome Congress's low approval ratings?
a) Focus on their punctuality
b) Change the meaning of the word "approval"
c) Accuse pollsters of encouraging terrorists
d) A generous donation to the polling lobby

What changes would you bring to Congress?
a) Higher pay for strategists
b) Altering the lineup in the annual volleyball tourney against the Senate
c) Rebranding with name change to "Awesome Patriot Hero House"
d) Mostly diaper

What might you name a bill that restricts minority voting rights?
a) The Rosa Parks Memorial Act
b) I Have a Dream II, for Reals This Time
c) The Even More Patriot-y Act
d) Hey Black Folks, Vote for This, It's Good for You

What is the primary role of the media in a democratic society?
a) Giving punctuation advice
b) Writing pithy headlines
c) Providing a constant stream of celebrity crotch-shots
d) It varies according to what I'm pimping

Where do you see the American government in 100 years?
a) Enjoying a lucrative endorsement deal with Exxon
b) Battling the zombie apocalypse
c) In Beijing
d) Underwater

Define "truth."
a) Perspective
b) Volume
c) Truth is in the eye of what I market to the beholder
d) Beauty is truth, truth beauty. Just kidding—follow the cash.

Application to Work at the Department of Motor Vehicles in Charlottesville, Virginia

WE AT THE Department of Motor Vehicles in Charlottesville, Virginia, pride ourselves on selecting employees most suited to DMV work culture. Candidates from motor vehicle departments around the country transfer here to become leaders in the field of frustrating the people who pay our salaries. Be warned, the selection process is arduous, as only the most bitter and incompetent applicants find a home in our office. And by "home," we mean eight hours a day of creating a hell on earth for innocent customers. Please fill out the following form to get started.

How would you describe your attitude?
a) Surly
b) Very surly
c) I fully expect to die at work every day
d) You do *not* want to get me started

What disgusts you most about DMV customers?
a) They exist
b) Their annoying habit of standing in the wrong line for hours like I told them to

c) Their mistake-catching abilities
d) Prioritizing their preschool pickup over my hourly coffee break

What amazing feats can you accomplish with eight-inch fingernails?
a) I can hold a phone and still scratch my crotch
b) I can dial phone numbers with a nine-inch pencil
c) I can type at five words per minute without a chip
d) I can point a customer to the next line by touching the next line

What made you want to join the DMV?
a) I was bullied as a child
b) I was bullied in high school
c) I was bullied as an adult
d) I like being a bully

What original methods have you devised for torturing customers?
a) When I call their name I make it sound like an insult
b) I force them to stand in line for an hour to pick up a form that should be available online or in a rack by the door
c) I send important notices to their old address on purpose
d) I sharpen the paper clips and paint the tips with curare

If you could have any other job, what would it be?
a) Sith Lord
b) Anger Management Instigator
c) Lion Shamer
d) Monsanto Lobbyist

What's your favorite color?
a) The color of despair
b) Black like Dick Cheney's soul
c) Whatever color Sauron likes
d) Colors are for happy people

What causes you the most pain?
a) Kittens
b) Rainbows
c) Helping people
d) Natural light

APPENDIX B
CANADIAN GLOSSARY

Get to know your new leader's language
....

ALL-DRESSED (n.): Dressing with the implicit intention of attracting the opposite (or same) sex. *Also* (food): the works; the whole nine yards of available toppings; difficult to discern individual flavors, but still good: *Been a long winter, sis? You look like a whore, all-dressed like that.*

BACHELOR (n.): A no-bedroom apartment, usually occupied by a writer, an actor, or the creator of a fringe political party: *You must be so lonely in this bachelor. Are those your cats?*

BEAVER BREATH (n.): The taste and smell of one's mouth the morning after drinking at least 50 percent of a two-four: *I love you baby, but you have some serious beaver breath.*

BEAVER TAIL (n.): The tail on a North American beaver. (What did you think it was?): *That beaver has a beaver tail.*

CANCON (n.): Short for "Canadian Content," a law requiring broadcasters to air a certain percentage of made-in-Canada programming. The policy is useful for getting children to play outside by preventing excessive quality on Canadian television: *Hey,* Little Mosque on the Prairie *is on! I'll get the sticks, you set up the net.*

CANUCK (prop. n.): A member of Vancouver's elite hockey posse. *Also* (n.): a term of unity for Canadians: *We are all Canucks. Except Greg—he's a dick.*

CBC (prop. n.): The Canadian Broadcasting Corporation. Similar to America's PBS, minus the excessive funding: *The CBC found a toonie in its pocket, doubling the number of shows it can produce this year.*

CHEEZIES (n.): Small, crunchy, artificially cheese-flavored bits of air. Commonly found at convenience stores and in the laps of high people: *I could eat a bag of Cheezies, right now, all by myself. Or seven bags.*

CHESTERFIELD (n.): A loveseat that has been welded into a mega-loveseat to accommodate three to six adult Canadians. *Also* (v.): The movement of a chesterfield onto the patio the moment summer arrives: *It's ten degrees Celsius, time to chesterfield. I'll get the sunscreen.*

CURLING (n.): The official Canadian sport for people who don't like sports: *I'm too drunk to play Frisbee golf. Let's go curling.*

DICK-ALL (n.): Nothing; shit-all, done through lack of will, stubbornness, or intoxication: *The government is doing dick-all about the glowing ducks in that tailings pond.*

EH (interjection): The Canadian equivalent of punctuation: *No worries, eh.*

FORTY-NINTH PARALLEL (n.): The Canadian equivalent of the Mexican border: *I wish these immigrants would stop crossing the forty-ninth parallel to steal our jobs.*

FORTY-POUNDER (n.): The default weight chosen when lying about fish size. *Also* (n.): a forty-fluid-ounce bottle of liquor (Canadian rye, rum, vodka, or gin—but not beer): *Went ice-fishing last week, me and the boys killed a forty-pounder and caught two or three, probably, forty-pounders.*

GAUNCH/GITCH/GINCH (n.): Underwear—long, boxer, brief, or thong: *I pulled his gaunch/gitch/ginch so high he could taste his own undercarriage.*

GOOSE TRAP (n.): Where two or more ex-girlfriends simultaneously approach from different sides of the room. Frequently occurs in Canada because everyone knows Ian from Toronto: *Bridget and Sophie totally pulled a goose trap on me at the pub. Turns out they were in Girl Guides together.*

HOCKEY (n.): A Canadian sport, pastime, season, way of life, and all-purpose excuse for getting out of anything: *Why did you schedule our wedding during a preseason junior hockey exhibition scrimmage?*

HOLLYWOOD NORTH (prop. n.): Vancouver's film community, where every science fiction film and television series of the past decade was shot: *Hollywood North converted my office into a Cylon base.**

HOSER (n.): *See also* "shit disturber." An innocuous way to refer to someone who is being a bit dickish or difficult, or is drinking all of your beer. *Also* (rural): One who, when intoxicated, takes pleasure in peeing on a friend or acquaintance (it is considered un-Canadian to urinate on strangers): *Melissa must have drank that whole forty-pounder. Looks like the hoser is setting up to hit Pete.*

HYDRO (n.): The Canadian term for electricity, which is largely supplied by hydroelectric power: *I can't pay the hydro this month because I'm watching hockey.*

LOONIE (n.): A one-dollar coin whose value fluctuates with the maple syrup market: *Can you spot me a loonie to buy some maple syrup?*

MICKEY (n.): A discreet, pocket-sized bottle containing thirteen fluid ounces of liquor, suitable for concerts, expensive sporting events, inexpensive sporting events, outdoor events, indoor events, snow skiing, high-school dances, glove boxes, office drawers, briefcases, backpacks, and just about anywhere one might conceal a handgun: *If you need a quick pinch, there is a mickey of rye under the car seat.*

MOUNTIE (prop. n.): A member of the Royal Canadian Mounted Police. *Also* (n.): One who is being mounted: *Stay*

---

* This actually happened to one of us.

away from that Mountie's Taser, or he will make you his mountie.

NEWFIE (prop. n.): A member of a strangely delightful and lovable people who live in, or are from, the province of Newfoundland. Also known as the Canadian Oompa-Loompa, the Newfie has an accent that makes communicating nearly impossible (*see* America's Deep South). The phonetics of a Newfie sentence: *Wre y'at? Da ba! Tot we'd ld uät da truc n hed nôrt, fer d'nite. I'com'ta-bar, ode'on.*

PARKADE (n.): A multilevel, often subterranean parking lot: *Melanie and I used to bone in the parkade at night.*

PISSLE (n.): The amount of post-urinal drip needed to produce a visible pant spot of at least 3 centimeters (1.2 inches) in diameter. Frequently experienced when engaging in strong laughter with drunk friends: *Holy shit bro! Is that a pissle? Does that count? Let me get my ruler.*

ROUGHRIDER (prop. n.): A member of the Saskatchewan Roughriders or the Ottawa Rough Riders, who, incredibly, played in the Canadian Football League at the same time. *Also* (n.): A sexually aggressive Canadian woman: *That Saskatchewan roughrider popped my hip out of place.*

SHATNER (v.): The act of kicking one square in the testicles: *He fucking shatnered me!*

SHIT DISTURBER (n.): An individual who, after the fist fight, continues to mouth off and slander your girlfriend while everyone is trying to watch the film. *Also* (n.): A drunk friend who sneaks into your backyard and spreads out your dog's droppings to make tomorrow's collection more difficult: *Doug must have been drinking last night, the little shit disturber created a minefield out there.*

STAMPEDE (n.): Calgary's annual hat festival: *Are you going to this year's Stampede? No, I don't have a hat.*

TOBOGGAN (n.): A sled or sleighlike winter vehicle made of wood, plastic, metal, or garbage bags. Employed in the winter months for downhill sledding and keeping dentists employed: *I got shatnered by a toboggan!*

TOQUE (n.): A knit cap; Northern Christian yarmulke; frequently worn for survival during the cold winter months. More recently (urban), worn as a fashion statement in nonfrozen months or to display douchery when worn during an indoor workout: *Is that shit disturber wearing a toque while doing squats?*

TRANSCANADA (n.): The eight-thousand-kilometer (five-thousand-mile) highway connecting a string of places nobody wants to visit: *How the hell did we get onto the TransCanada?*

TWO-FOUR (n.): A box of twenty-four cans or bottles of beer. *Also* (n.): May 24, Queen Victoria's birthday, the holiday weekend that kicks off summer camping for most Canadians: *We have four bags of Cheezies, three two-fours, two mickeys, a forty-pounder, a Newfie, night toques, firewood, and a canoe. Let's party till we pissle.*

ACKNOWLEDGMENTS

THE AUTHORS WOULD like to thank the people who make our work possible and our lives worth living: Mary Anderson-Van Luven, Denise Calvert, Madeline Calvert, David Calvert, Margo Calvert, Tristan Kromer, Adam Weinstein, Jim and Jenny Bryan and their assorted Jedi, Mark Woodman, Ian Graham, Alvaro Rojas, Oleg Solo, Greg Martin, the Rio Theatre, the British Columbia Arts Council, the Canada Council for the Arts, Point Blank Creative, Zulu Records, the Tipper Restaurant, the *Bro Jake Show*, the *Tyee*, Jason Yarn, Scott McIntyre, Trena White, Emiko Morita, Alison Cairns, Peter Cocking, Richard Nadeau, Claire McKinney, Peter Norman, every last face at Douglas & McIntyre, and the unbound spirit of Robin Wheeler, whose heart was a continent.

Portions of this book have been printed in the *Tyee* (www.thetyee.ca) and broadcast on CFMI Vancouver.

CHRIS CANNON IS the author of five books and hundreds of articles in magazines such as *Rolling Stone, Men's Journal,* and the *Tyee.* A former U.S. Marine Corps sergeant, Chris served in the Presidential Honor Guard and in the intelligence and counterterrorism fields. He now teaches cultural criticism at the University of British Columbia. His work has received awards and grants from the Tides Foundation, the Western Magazine Awards, the Canada Council for the Arts, and the British Columbia Arts Council, and he is the recipient of the 2011 Dave Greber Award. He lives in Vancouver, B.C. www.cannonwriter.com

BRIAN CALVERT HAS written, acted, produced, directed, or edited over fifty short films and five multimedia (live and video) stage shows. He is cocreator of the online sketch comedy groups ChurchofJerks.com and VILLAGEiDiOT.ca. Brian completed much of his schooling in Sarnia, Ontario, border city to Port Huron, Michigan. He now lives in Vancouver. www.brianMcalvert.com